THE HORSE AND THE BLUE GRASS COUNTRY

THE HORSE AND THE

By BRADLEY SMITH

BLUE GRASS COUNTRY

DOUBLEDAY & COMPANY, INC., GARDEN CITY, NEW YORK

For Josie and Ed, my mother and father, who bought me a horse when I was nine years old.

DESIGNED BY JOSEPH P. ASCHERL
LIBRARY OF CONGRESS CATALOG CARD NUMBER 60–6502
COPYRIGHT © 1955, 1960, BY BRADLEY SMITH
ALL RIGHTS RESERVED
PRINTED IN THE UNITED STATES OF AMERICA

Contents

Foreword

THIS IS an unusual book about horses and about a unique land made famous by them. In story and picture, it covers the horses from birth to memorial headstones, and it covers the Blue Grass region of Kentucky from its legends and traditions to the rich beauty which makes the countryside charming for its many visitors.

When I first met the author, he was working with A. B. Guthrie—the Pulitzer prize winner was then a resident of Lexington—on a piece for Holiday magazine about the state of Kentucky. He told stories of the nights he and Bud stayed awake until dawn, sustained only by professional zeal and Bourbon whiskey, in order to greet a Thoroughbred foal as it was born and while it essayed its first unsteady steps—an event which, in central Kentucky, may be likened to the arrival of a new soul in Paradise.

Later, about five years ago, Bradley Smith returned to the Blue Grass as a *Life* essayist. I had lunch with him at the Coach House, and he has dropped in to see me on most of his visits since then.

On one of these visits to my office, he told me of his plans for this book. He wanted to make it a book, not only for "people interested in horses," but for people, whether interested in horses or not. I encouraged him, and not many months later I had the pleasure of reading the first draft of the typescript and seeing some of the pictures.

The author has sketched the Blue Grass country in terms of its traditions, past and present, with just enough detail concerning men and mansions to provide a glimpse of a culture whose emblem is a spindle-legged foal on a green background. He has laughed gently at some of the foibles of this region—the ones at which Kentuckians themselves are permitted to laugh. And he has repeated, for the benefit of posterity's current crop, a few passages of the sonorous rhetoric that flowed with the juleps of yesteryear. Moreover, he has given a recipe for burgoo.

I am glad that a photo-journalist with the experience and skill of Bradley Smith has turned his lenses, literal and figurative, upon the Blue Grass region.

J. A. ESTES
Editor of *The Blood-Horse*

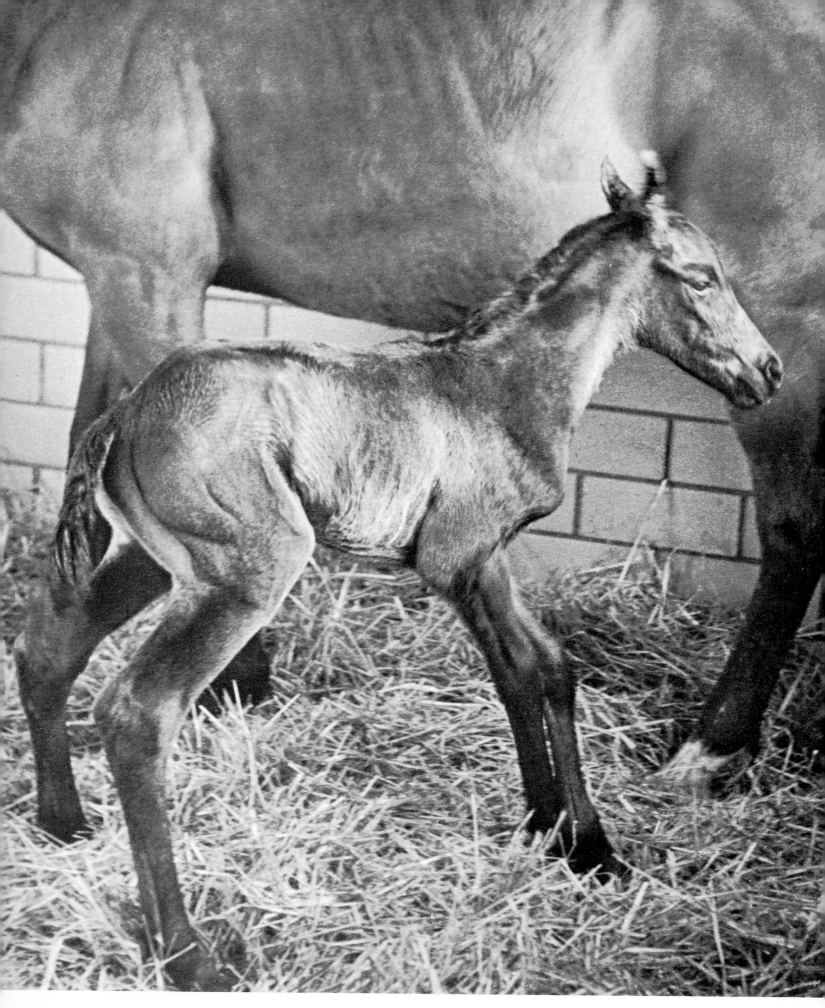

Only minutes old, this newborn foal stands up for the first time.

Introduction

THE BLUE GRASS COUNTRY is a parklike meadow covering twenty-four hundred square miles of fertile grasslands. Located in north central Kentucky this legendary green pasture has more statues to horses than to people. Its reputation for fast horses, beautiful women, virile men, and potent whisky is deserved, even if the adjectives do occasionally get mixed.

This is the home of the thoroughbred horse. With horizon to horizon carpeting, white filigree-lace fences, and palatial horse farms, it is the ideal spawning ground for more than $150,000,000 worth of speed and sport on the hoof each year.

The center of the Blue Grass area is the cultured city of Lexington, whose twenty-eight square miles include some eighty thousand horse lovers. From Lexington, extending outward for forty-five miles like the spokes of a wheel, is the "inner" Blue Grass, heart of the horse country.

But the Blue Grass region is more than a place where the *Poa pratensis* grass seed grows and where horses are foaled, broken, trained, schooled and raced. It is a country of tradition where great characters of the past and present, both human and animal, stroll by. The Marquis de Lafayette, a great horseman, tarried and gave his name to Fayette County; bourbon whiskey was born in the Blue Grass; Paris and Versailles are the two leading towns of the region after Lexington. It is the country of Daniel Boone who camped on Elkhorn Creek; of Henry Clay, who wagered at the old Lexington track; of *Aristides,* winner of the first Kentucky Derby; of *Man o' War* and *Nashua;* of *Volomite,* sire of the great trotters, and *Wing Commander,* king of the show horses. It is also a state of mind, a way of thinking that cannot be found anywhere else in the world.

But is the grass really blue? Some eminent Kentuckians say that in the spring, when the new grass is budding and the soft wind ripples the top layer, the undulating fields have a soft bluish cast. This is, however, debatable; the magical quality of the light, the reflection from the sky, and the sympathetic attitude of the viewer may be responsible. Technically, the blueness of the grass is a myth but everyone knows, especially in Kentucky, that myths and legends are more likely to be true than are facts.

This, then, is a book about the myths and legends, the cold facts and the warm stories about the fleet horses, great houses, and the uninhibited characters of the Blue Grass country.

Getting acquainted on day of foaling, a contented dam examines her offspring.

Mares and Foals

IT IS 4 A.M. on a fresh, cool spring morning. The yellow-white glow of the bare electric bulbs is shining, wreathed in a halo, through the foggy night as the moon sets back of the quiet barn. You drive closer and your mist-dimmed headlights reveal the new station wagon of the farm manager. He is on hand at this hour because it is time for the birth of a thoroughbred.

Eleven months of careful preparation have preceded this hour. The dam has been prudently exercised, her feed has been supplemented with vitamins and molasses. Every effort has been made to keep her free of colic and digestive disturbances, and now she is in the comfortably equipped foaling barn, the maternity ward of the horse farm.

Within the scrubbed barn you meet the watchman and the "foaling man," a methodical, patient, experienced character who has attended the birth rites of

Ready to go out into the sunshine, newborn foal is helped by groom.

hundreds of colts. The mare is pacing nervously up and down in the large special stall strewn with sweet-smelling hay. The farm manager, who lives in his clothing like a fireman during this spring season because most foals are "dropped" at night, watches her carefully. "Won't be long now," he says over his shoulder. "Her bag is full and the milk is coming fast." The mare is beginning to "steam" as her body temperature goes up just before the birth. She may get up, lie down, and then get up again, but before dawn her pedigreed son or daughter will be beside her.

The foal is born in the position of a diver. The front legs are pointed forward, the long furry head against and almost between them. By this time the foaling man is in the stall, assisting if necessary. He may pull a bit on the forelegs and when the colt emerges open the sac that surrounds it. Most foals come easily in this normal fashion but sometimes a leg may be folded back or it may come upside down. In these cases the vet is immediately called, but the foaling man, meanwhile, tries to straighten things out, to turn him over or to arrange the bent leg in a better position. Foals rarely come backward and then, even with the vet on hand, there is usually serious trouble and often the foal must be destroyed to save the life of the dam.

But this one has no trouble, and a few minutes after the forelegs have appeared, the long slim body and then the hind legs, also extended, are visible. The umbilical cord breaks naturally when the mare rises, and the attendant quickly applies antiseptic to the navel. The dam, still nervous and exhausted, is curious and carefully examines her offspring, then begins to clean it up a bit.

If all is well, the foal will stand by himself and begin to nurse within the hour. This is the time of greatest tension for the watchers, for now the newborn is entirely on his own. He must learn to stand by himself and to find his mother's milk. Unless he does this within the first three hours at most, there is something wrong and the chances are exceedingly high that, if he lives, he is not likely to amount to much. On some farms, after the foal rises, the attendant will help him find the dam's bag and get him started nursing. This is sometimes necessary with a maiden mare having her first foal, for she will sometimes kick her foal when he first tries to nurse.

Unlike human births, no one is much concerned about the weight of the newborn. The big questions are: how soon will it stand up, how active is it in nursing, and does it seem lively and well formed. As he grows into a suckling, weanling, and yearling, his growth, eating habits, and social behavior will be constantly observed.

Now he has an identity. He may be a chestnut with a white blaze or a smaller star on his forehead and possibly white stockings, or a bay with black points (black on lower legs, mane, and tail), or a Black or Brown. It is much less likely that he will be a Gray, Dun, or Roan, for less than five per cent of all the thoroughbred foals come in these lighter colors. But although he can be identified by color, he will be called a foal until after his first birthday, which is January first for all thoroughbreds. During his first seven to nine months, beginning the first day, he will be in continuous contact with man. Every horse farm has a man whose specialty is taking care of the foals. He has a halter ready the first time the foal is allowed out and then makes a point of handling the same foal every day. Thoroughbreds are naturally temperamental and wild and they are likely to kick or bite the hand that feeds them. When they lose contact with man, they become very difficult to manage.

Within twenty-four hours, weather permitting, the foal and his mother will be out in the warm Blue Grass country sunshine. There in a protected paddock the mare will graze over the gently rolling hills while she teaches her foal to exercise. If it lies down too much she nudges or gently kicks it; if it nurses too slowly she pokes at its bottom with her head, pushing it closer to her teats. She will run along the undulating white fences, always keeping just far enough away to make her youngster run to catch up.

Leggy thoroughbred foal nurses at his patient dam on Mereworth Farm.

15

Mare and foal graze peacefully at Calumet Farm near Lexington, Kentucky.

Adventurous youngster reaches out for delicate leaves over fence.

This picture is repeated throughout the Blue Grass area every year from February through April. During these spring months the horse country is happily reborn as a new crop of three thousand (more or less) spindle-legged, fur-soft, awkward, fleet-footed shy nurslings trot and gallop over the lush meadows or lie on the tender new grass soaking up the sunshine.

Meanwhile the dam is leading an easy, well-tended life. But, because of her great value as a mother of potential winning race horses, she is often bred again just nine days after foaling. She may be carrying one foal while educating the other. A really good mare, the dam of a distinguished stakes winner, is known as a producer. She has also been referred to as a running gold mine. But perhaps the greatest compliment is the breeder's boast: "When *she* drops a foal it hits the ground running." There is also the story about the fleet Kentucky mare that was entered in an out-of-state race back in the eighties. She was ten-months pregnant but, at the starting bell, was off like a shot before the other horses had gotten started. Halfway around the track, she stopped, it is said, and had her foal. Then, as the other horses passed, she got up, took off, and won the race. Her foal finished second, of course.

But our foal is not racing yet, not even considering it. His days are spent in leisurely growth. At three days old he will start nibbling at hay; at three weeks

17

Foals are born with legs so long they have trouble reaching down to the Blue Grass.

Lazing in the sun, newborn foals, like newborn babies, mostly sleep and eat.

he will have his own feed tub and start learning to eat grain. Mare and foal are always fed separately because the dam will chase him away if he attempts to eat with her.

She will nurse him from six to eight months, or even longer unless he is weaned. The weaning process is a delicate one. The foals have learned to depend on their dams and when they are suddenly on their own, they become tense and overactive. Most of the Blue Grass horse farms put the weanlings in individual stalls, next to one another, and take the mares away. Then, after giving them time to simmer down, a couple of the least promising may be let out to "run down." They will gallop at breakneck speed and may hurt themselves. When the first out have calmed down, the others are let out. Foals are highly imitative, and the others will run at a less dangerous clip.

In the months since his birth our foal has become almost as tall as his dam; he weighs from five to seven hundred pounds, and by the time he becomes a well-grown one-year-old, the lights in the maternity barn are burning late again and the foaling man is getting ready for the next crop of brand-new Kentucky thoroughbreds.

The Development of the Horse

FROM THE BEGINNING of recorded history, even in the earliest cave drawings, the horse has been important in the push of civilization. So it was in the early days in the Blue Grass country.

When Daniel Boone rode into the Blue Grass region following the trail of John Finley, Thomas Walker, and Christopher Gist, he knew from their explorations that the "Kentateh" of the Chickasaw Indians was more than a "dark and bloody ground." On April 1, 1775, Boone settled on Otter Creek near the present village of Boonesboro. His resourcefulness and courage gave confidence to the new settlers who followed.

These pioneers were resolute and intrepid. Among them were Revolutionary War generals with land grants; ordinary soldiers, impatient to explore and own new land; French engineers; Dutch farmers from Pennsylvania, and settlers from Virginia and the Carolinas who came with their slaves and their British-based culture. Captain Gilbert Imlay of the Revolutionary War later wrote of the land of these settlers, "Everything here assumes a dignity and splendor I have never seen in any part of the world. Here an eternal verdure reigns and the brilliant sun of latitude thirty-nine degrees, piercing through the azure heavens, produces in the prolific soil an early maturity which is truly astonishing."

The settlers brought their horses, or rather, their horses brought them. They were not adventurers or trappers but, for the most part, farmers and stockbreeders. These self-sufficient men and women knew, along with work, how to study and to play.

Their greatest recreation was the racing of their horses. Even before Kentucky became a state, and before Lexington was founded, there were races on the main street of this frontier village. The races became so frequent and were so well attended that they disrupted the town's affairs, and finally the city fathers were forced to pass an ordinance forbidding them in the village streets.

In 1816 an early Kentucky historian, Mann Butler, wrote, "Every young man I know has a horse, a gun, and a violin," which indicates that a pattern of Kentucky culture was forming even then.

The horse was an important foundation stone of this pattern. Even though this animal was not native to the Western Hemisphere, it had in the early dawn of mammal life, but as quite another form of horse, roamed the plains of the United States. There was little resemblance between *Eohippus,* the first horse, and the thoroughbred that evolved millions of years later to its present state in Kentucky. This first horselike animal completely disappeared from the Americas. Whether primitive man hunted and destroyed him or whether some natural catastrophe was responsible for his extinction we do not know. But we do know that *Eohippus* was about the size of a small greyhound and had a tiny skull, well-padded hoofs, three toes on his hind feet and four on the front. Though not much to look at, *Eohippus* was alert and adaptable. He survived in Europe and Asia, but not in the Western Hemisphere.

A few million years later, as *Mesohippus,* he was longer and heavier and almost as big as a collie. Next, as *Parahippus,* he had a longer head and longer legs and looked somewhat like the horse we know. Survival at this time was difficult, and *Parahippus* was followed by *Merychippus,* who was the size of a small pony. Finally *Pliohippus,* the direct ancestor of *Equus,* appeared. It doesn't take long to tell this story but it took more than sixty million years from tiny *Eohippus* to *Equus,* the glacial horse that has survived to the present time.

Historically it is a short stretch from the glacial horse to the present thoroughbred. He got his start in Spain early in the twelfth century. Knights in heavy armor used big-boned heavy horses that were powerful but slow. But warfare on horseback proved that the Moors with their quick, fast-running Barbary and Arabian horses could and did outfight and outrun knights on their slower bulky animals.

The crusaders and indeed all the fighting men of Europe learned this lesson quickly. As early as the reign of William the Conqueror, Barb and Arab horses were imported into England and bred to native stock. Thus the taproot mares of England, which would a few centuries later again be served by Barb and Arab stallions, were created. These mares were destined one day to begin the line of thoroughbreds that come down to the fleet Kentucky racers of today.

Meanwhile, as a result of the development of the large, agile, speedy horse, a revolution in riding techniques was taking place. Because the Barb and Arab horses were lighter as well as faster, the heavy iron and leather saddles were replaced by lighter all-leather gear. Horsemanship became so important in Spain that the word "caballero," which meant horseman, was used to denote "a gentleman" even as it is today. And these new-style, faster-riding gentlemen on their agile but sturdy mounts were about to undertake the conquest of the New World.

Columbus brought to the New World the first horses since the long-extinct *Eohippus.* After his second voyage he wrote to Luis de Santanger of the Spanish court that the recently discovered lands offered fine pasturage and climate for the breeding of horses. In his four voyages Columbus delivered approximately one hundred horses to the New World. In 1494 he wrote, "Each time there is sent here (to Santo Domingo) any type of boat there should be included some brood mares." In 1500, due to his persistence, a breeding ranch with sixty brood mares was established on Hispaniola. Later, Hernán Cortés, venturing into the southwestern regions of North America, found that his horses had much to do with the success of the conquest. The Indians were both more frightened and impressed by the horses than by the soldiers. From these horses and others imported by later Spanish explorers, the western mustang and cow pony spring.

But it took more than one hundred fifty years from the time of Columbus for the true thoroughbred line to be born in England. Three great stallions became the foundation of a line that stretches from seventeenth-century England to twentieth-century Kentucky. Every thoroughbred can trace his pedigree back to one of three great English horses.

Captain Byerly had a "charging horse" which he rode in the Irish Wars. This stallion was probably a mixture of Persian, Arab, and Barb blood, and while at stud sired some of the fastest runners of his time. He founded the line of the *Byerly Turk.* Most important of his get was *Herod,* a great-great-grandson, foaled in 1758.

No one is quite sure how Lord Godolphin came into possession of his handsome Arabian stallion. Some horse historians say he was a gift to King Louis XIV of France from the Sultan of Morocco. Others say he was a present from the Bey of Tunis. There is still another story that he was stolen in France and spirited away to England. Nevertheless, existing records show that he became the most important stallion in the stud of the Earl of Godolphin. He founded the line of the *Godolphin Arabian* and his most famous offspring was *Matchem,* foaled in 1748.

There is no mystery about the origin of the famous stallion of Mr. Darley of Yorkshire. Darley's son Thomas, while in Aleppo, Syria, bought a bay stallion and sent it home to his father. The handsome horse stood fifteen hands high and arrived in England at the age of four years. He became generally known as the *Darley Arabian* and was the great-great-grandfather of *Eclipse* (who was born on a day when the sun was darkened), from which the majority of the thoroughbred racers of today trace their lineage.

While there are many romantic stories about the first three great stallions, the stories told of the *Godolphin Arabian* are by far the most interesting. It is said that he fought a vicious, biting, kicking battle with *Hobgoblin,* another stallion of the day, for possession of the mare *Roxana.* Whether or not the battle occurred, early stud records show that the *Godolphin Arabian* was indeed mated to *Roxana* and that the resulting foal, *Lath,* became a legendary runner of his day.

Today the only descendants of the *Byerly Turk, Godolphin,* and *Darley Arabian* that have survived come through their illustrious progeny, *Herod, Matchem,* and *Eclipse.*

On the female side, or tail female line, the picture is not so clear. The three foundation stallions were undoubtedly bred to as many native and imported mares as possible. The mares were selected for their speed and appearance. Only about forty of these can be identified in the earliest records. Identification is complicated further because mares in the early days, and even up to 1800 in Kentucky, were called by the name of their sire or by the owner of the stallion. For instance, *Mare from the Morocco Barb* or *Mare by T. Gascoign's Foreign Horse.*

So for almost a hundred years thoroughbred breeding continued in England. The finest stallions were bred to the best available mares. Racing had existed for

EOHIPPUS

Eohippus was the tiny first horse that lived in the Eocene period forty million years ago. His teeth were low-crowned, like the deer. He had four toes on his front feet, only three on the rear.

MESOHIPPUS

Mesohippus lived in the Oligocene period about thirty million years ago. More like a horse and less like a large dog, he was distinguished by three toes on each foot with the middle one the most prominent.

Neohipparion belonged to the Pliocene period some ten million years ago. His teeth had become longer, allowing him to eat tough grasses. His middle toe was quite prominent, the others less useful.

Equus Scotti was the horse of the more recent Pleistocene, thousands rather than millions of years ago. He had only one large toe like the horse's hoof today. Although smaller he was much like today's horse.

Boston was won in a card game called "Boston" and became the fleetest racer of his day. When he was sixteen years old he sired *Lexington* who was foaled after his death in 1850.

centuries on an informal basis. It had been an event in the twenty-third Olympiad in Greece, which was held in the late seventh century B.C. Slowly, through its long history, racing became formalized. In 1780 the first English Derby was held at Epsom. Its winner contributed greatly not only to racing in England but was later to have an important effect on all the thoroughbreds in the United States.

The winner was *Diomed*, named for King Diomedes of Thrace. It was on his island that Hercules fought the man-eating mares. *Diomed*, in his Derby year, outran all the thoroughbreds of England. He was, however, retired after only a few years of racing and was not considered a good sire by the British. Late in his life he came to America and there sired the great *Sir Archie* out of the blind mare, *Castianira*, on the pleasant Virginia farm, Mount Airy, owned by John Tayloe.

But *Diomed* was by no means the first thoroughbred stallion to be brought to the Americas. That honor traditionally goes to *Bulle Rock*, who was imported late in life by Samuel Gist, an ancestor of one of Kentucky's first settlers. *Bulle Rock* was far less successful a stallion than *Diomed*, and his line disappeared after a few

24

Lexington begot more first-class horses than any American stallion. He was sixteen times the number-one stallion in the United States. He sired a total of 543 foals, mostly fine racers.

generations. Other famous early importations were *Monkey* and *Traveller* (who arrived in 1749 and is not to be confused with General Robert E. Lee's Civil War horse). By 1760 racing had become an important institution in the eastern states. Even during the Revolutionary War, race meets were held on Long Island. Here the first racecourse in the United States was laid out at Hempstead Plains and called Newmarket after the course of King James I.

Before and during the Revolutionary War such distinguished Americans as George Washington participated actively in racing. Washington was a racing steward in Alexandria, Virginia, in 1761. After the war, rivalry in the racing world between the North and South was intense. Baltimore became a center for great match races between northern and southern thoroughbreds.

Then as the war ended there was a small migration to the West. The Blue Grass region was discovered and the sons and daughters of *Bulle Rock, Monkey,* and the great *Sir Archie* gradually migrated to north central Kentucky and down into Tennessee.

Glencoe was bred in England by Lord Jersey and considered the "best horse in the world" after winning the Ascot Gold Cup. He stood at stud at Blue Grass Farms late in his life.

A blending of unparalleled elements made the Blue Grass region the utopian breeding ground for thoroughbreds. First there was the land, a long rippling pasturage with hills sloping just enough to exercise properly the growing colts and fillies. But the maturing horses needed more than rolling terrain; they needed the kind of food that would build durable bones and powerful muscles. The northeast section of Kentucky was made to order. A unique outcropping of Ordovician limestone, located at what the geologists call the Cincinnati anticline, made the soil rich in phosphorus and calcium, just what the thoroughbreds needed to develop a comparatively lightweight framework that would withstand the bone-shattering pounding of racing at top speed. Kentucky farmers say the soil is so rich that if you plant a nail at night it will come up a spike in the morning. Fortunately the subsoil was porous enough to prevent the area from becoming boggy or swampy, for the horses needed firm ground to develop strong leg bones and firm feet.

Kentucky was one of the most celebrated runners of the '60s. He was bred by John M. Clay, the son of Henry Clay. His sire was the noted *Lexington* and his dam *Magnolia*, by *Glencoe*.

Now add another component, the high mineral content of meandering Elkhorn Creek water. This useful stream still winds in and out of the horse farms, adding beauty as well as utility to the countryside.

Climate is also important. Horse-breeding experts everywhere agree that the weather of the Blue Grass is just about faultless. Winters are just nippy enough to keep horses hardy and weatherproof and yet not long enough to keep them out of the body-building sunshine. Because the summers are long, foals dropped in the spring are big enough and tough enough by late fall to withstand the winter cold.

Visual proof of the efficacy of the diet, water, climate, and pasturage may be seen at the Smithsonian Institution, where the massive skeleton of *Lexington,* greatest of the Blue Grass stallions, is preserved.

Finally, one more element was added to the winning combination of terrain, soil, water, and climate. This was the nature of the Kentuckians themselves. Cultured, yet adventurous, vigorous, enterprising, and volatile, they loved life

*DIOMED chestnut 1777
  by Florizel – sister to Juno, by Spectator

SIR ARCHY brown 1805
  by *Diomed – *Castianira, by Rockingham

TIMOLEON chestnut 1813
  by Sir Archy – mare by *Saltram

BOSTON chestnut 1833
  by Timoleon – mare by Ball's Florizel

LEXINGTON brown 1850
  by Boston – Alice Carneal, by *Sarpedon

AEROLITE chestnut mare 1861
  by Lexington – Florine, by *Glencoe

---

and they loved horses. There was a saying that if a man did not like horses, no matter where he happened to be born, he was not a Kentuckian. Horses to them were not a means of transportation but a way of life. They were their business and also their recreation. Greatest of all activities was horse racing. Meets were held on the savannas, in the dusty streets of the towns, and on the primitive tracks. Even in the days of frequent Indian raids race meetings were held. During the year 1788 the *Kentucky Gazette* carried this paid announcement:

CHART

SPENDTHRIFT *chestnut 1876*
  *by *Australian – Aerolite, by Lexington*

HASTINGS *brown 1893*
  *by Spendthrift – *Cinderella, by Blue Ruin or Tomahawk*

FAIR PLAY *chestnut 1905*
  *by Hastings – *Fairy Gold, by Bend Or*

MAN O' WAR *chestnut 1917*
  *by Fair Play – Mahubah, by *Rock Sand*

WAR ADMIRAL *brown 1934*
  by Man o' War – Brushup, by Sweep

x indicates foreign bred horses

Notice is hereby given that several gentlemen propose a meeting at the

CRAB ORCHARD on the 4th of July

in perfect readiness to move early the next morning through the wilderness.

As it is very dangerous on account of the Indians

it is hoped each person will go well armed.

Whirlaway was excellent example of modern horse but was not a successful sire.

So with constant care and highly selective breeding the thoroughbred thrived. There was a setback while the War of 1812 was fought. For almost ten years racing languished. Then came a great upsurge of interest in breeding and in racing. The Kentucky Association was formed in 1826, and such men as Henry Clay, who owned a number of thoroughbreds, and Dr. Elisha Warfield, breeder of *Lexington,* were active sportsmen of the day. Clay, then at the height of his career as a politician, gave his string of horses to his son, John M. Clay, who became an important horse breeder for the next half century.

In 1837 William P. Fessenden accompanied Daniel Webster on his visit to Lexington, and wrote, "We arrived here at exactly the right season to see the last of the spring races. Four horses were entered. I lost eight hailstorms (drinks) on *Maria Louisa.* The Kentuckians, as you are probably aware, value themselves greatly in their breed of horses, and enter into the spirit of such an occasion, and it is not disagreeable to see such men as Clay, Crittenden, Robinson and others of that stamp apparently as much excited, talking as loudly, betting as freely, drinking as deeply and swearing as excessively as the jockeys themselves.

"A hailstorm is a brandy julep, a snowstorm is a weaker one. The way they drink those things in Kentucky is a caution to sinners."

Then came the Civil War. As Kentucky tried to remain neutral, the region was overrun by the armies of both the North and South. Many great horses, stallions, and brood mares were pressed into the service of their masters or seized by the enemy. Some of the important stallions of Woodburn Farm, then one of the region's most important breeding establishments, were shipped to Illinois for safety. At least one stallion was stolen by guerrillas. A posse from Woodburn traced and recaptured it.

During the war, racing continued, and after it was over, the Blue Grass settled into its place as the great thoroughbred center of the United States. Later, when racing was threatened by lack of controls, leading to frauds and chicanery,

Bull Lea, the great sire of modern times, faces his own statue at Calumet Farm.

the Kentucky State Legislature took over the regulation of the tracks. When this legislation was attacked in 1906, Judge Edward C. O'Rear wrote a memorable opinion lauding the virtues of the horse, "He bore his master on his journeys of business and state, his mistress on her missions of worship and social duty. Whether as a charger bearing the knight, or the palfry, my lady, or old Dobbin at the plough, he was more or less constantly associated with man as his dependable servant, intelligent companion and 'friend in need.' It is no wonder he had the care and attention prompted by gratitude, pride, and self-interests. He needs to be a good horse to well serve a busy master. Selection naturally followed from observation of desirable qualities, the best being kept to perpetuate their kind. He excelled his contemporaries, the ox and the ass, not so much in strength as in speed, beauty and endurance. His capabilities were more extensive. Living without recreation would be a hard if not unnatural lot. Even the Puritans found it so. The innocent amusements of a people are proper subjects for encouragement. . . . If the old adage be true that 'all work and no play makes Jack a dull boy,' it is equally true that all play and no work makes Jack a poor man. The happy medium is the safest lot. Among the recreations of the English-speaking people for many centuries has been that of horse racing. It takes a good horse to run a good race. The tests of strength, fleetness and endurance and intelligence have been the means by which the quality of the horse had been established.

". . . notwithstanding we live in an age of machinery and of mechanical motors, the horse has lost none of his ancient hold upon the admiration of men, and is found to be as much in demand, if not as indispensable, as ever he was. Nothing that has been and is yet the subject of such general interest and utility can be regarded as beyond the legitimate concern of the legislator."

Today the thoroughbred has come of age in the Blue Grass country. He has increased in size from approximately fourteen to sixteen hands, some six to eight inches. He can easily outrun the Arabs from which he sprang. He is probably more temperamental, too, but what can you expect of an animal that has associated with four generations of Kentuckians?

Well-grown yearling grazes; mare is in background.

The Yearlings

THE GREATEST SPECTATOR sport in the Blue Grass country and one of the most pleasant spectator sports in the world is watching the yearlings during the spring and summer months as they play like a group of school children at lunchtime. Their curiosity is boundless. The yearling examines every fence post, every tree, and every other yearling in his group. He also likes to stand on his hind legs and box and, occasionally, in his rough housing, to wrestle. He behaves like a young untrained athlete, which is what he is. In the weeks to come he will receive the kind of training that will make him a trim, hard-muscled, well-trained professional racer.

Watching the yearlings, and everyone who goes near the Blue Grass farms does, reveals that like first graders there are all kinds. The belligerent ones kick and snap at the timid ones; the sulky ones hang back and make no attempt to keep up with the others. Nips on the neck and short quick kicks are so rapid it takes a trained observer to follow the motion. This horseplay is important to the development of the yearlings. When they run and wheel around, they learn balance; as they rear on their hind legs, boxing with one another, they strengthen the all-important joints and tendons that will carry them on the track.

Although it's time now for them to go to school, they don't start classes until, in the horseman's parlance, they have been "broken." This is an unfortunate word, because the pre-school training of thoroughbred yearlings does anything but break their spirit. They are brought along quietly and carefully like champion tennis players or fine swimmers. Thoroughbreds can be led but they cannot be forced. Highly sensitive, they can be ruined in an instant by a thoughtless or brutal exercise boy or trainer. Yearlings learn fast; more intelligent than the average cold-blooded horse, the thoroughbred reacts to handling very quickly.

Pre-school training for these high-strung youngsters starts with the groom. The groom is essential. He is the man who has handled the horse from birth and has become a friend the foal has learned to trust. This friend stood by him while his hoofs were being trimmed (this has been done from the age of six weeks to keep them level), who protected him from colds and colic, who wormed him regularly, fed him vitamins, and saw that he had sweet feed (oats and molasses) and good hay before him. It's been a busy year for the groom. He's had to cope with not only the bad habits that foals easily develop but also with the various kinds of appetites. In horse-training talk a "good doer" is good to have around. A "poor doer" does not eat his food properly, much like a pouting two-year-old child. These habits form the beginning of the yearling's social life. For it is the responsibility of the groom to see that he will ultimately be able to mix with other horses on the track without kicking, crowding, or biting, but will behave like a two-year-old gentleman and a thoroughbred scholar.

Meanwhile his owner has selected a name for him. This is a major project and is not as easy as it might seem. Before any horse is raced, his name must be registered with the Jockey Club. In addition to the name, all identifying markings (blaze, spots, stockings), scars, and color accompany registration of the yearling's name. To keep the names distinctive the Jockey Club has made a series of intriguing rules. No trade or advertising names and no names of celebrated race horses may be used. To use the name of any previous horse it is necessary for the horse to have been dead fifteen years or more. The name may be three words or less but it cannot consist of more than sixteen letters and spaces. No yearling may be named for a friend of the owner or for any celebrity without an affidavit from this person approving the use of his name. No profane or suggestive names may be used, although a few doubles-entendres have slipped by the authorities. Breeders have always had great sport naming horses. A fleet runner of the eighteenth century was surprisingly called *Pot-8-Os*. Later such names as *Elastic* and *Macaroni* were used to designate leading racers.

But let's go back to the yearling's pre-schooling. The groom is the link between the yearling and the trainer who directs his education, which starts quietly within his stall in the barn. Then, while the groom continues to quiet the youngster, an

Almost ready for the yearling sales, Mereworth youngster gets final polishing.

exercise boy lays a light pad on his back and fastens it loosely around his middle with a surcingle. The yearling is likely to buck like a rodeo horse. The groom leads him slowly around the stall until they "get the jump out." Each day the girth is tightened a bit and, while there may be more bucking, after a few days the yearling is willing to wear pad and surcingle.

But on some of the horse farms "breaking" does not get this far. Some thoroughbred breeders are primarily in the horse-selling rather than in the horse-racing business. Instead of training, breaking, and schooling the yearlings, they keep them inside for safety and fattening for the annual yearling sales. So some yearlings are not given a chance to develop their real racing potential, but will look sleek and pretty at the summer auctions. Many that are going to the market will not get pushed around by other yearlings, which might do them a lot of good in their racing career. They will have their own paddock and will be put out only

Active yearlings cavort, wrestle, run and frolic across the Blue Grass pastures.

Curious yearlings watch every passer-by. They are gentle because of daily handling.

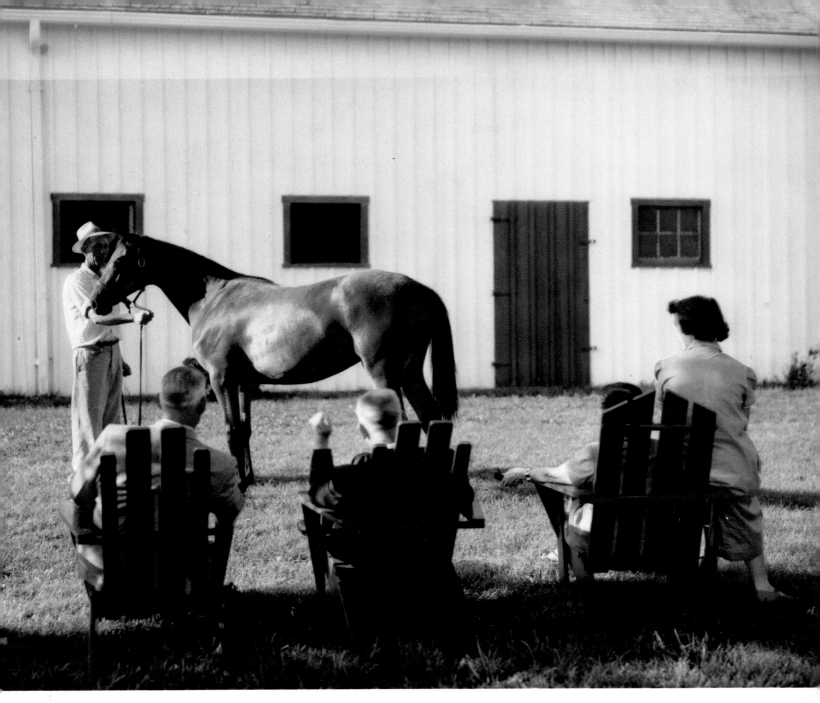

On a sunny Sunday afternoon, Dr. Asbury of Forest Retreat shows off a fine yearling to visitors.

in the early morning and late afternoon to keep the sun, which would also be good for them, from burning and deadening the appearance of their shining satin coats.

Getting yearlings ready for the sales is like getting horses into condition for a race. They must be in top physical condition; their feed must consist of special mixtures; and their grooming and handling cannot be done too carefully. The investment is too great for any chance-taking.

Each spring and fall in the United States the great yearling sales for thoroughbreds are held at the Keeneland racecourse in Lexington, Kentucky, and at Saratoga Springs, New York. As much as $10,000,000 change hands at the summer and fall auctions. Of course, in addition to this, a considerable number of yearlings are sold privately for prices ranging from $1,000 to $50,000. Individual

Looking like a champion, yearling struts before buyers at annual Keeneland auction. On the platform is low-pressure salesman, George Swinebroad, Lexington's top auctioneer. Audience includes representatives of the best racing stables of the nation.

After the yearling sales, a recalcitrant colt objects to being loaded into van.

yearlings have brought above $80,000 during recent years. Only occasionally do these high-priced yearlings return anything like their original investment. But old-timers like to point to *Alsab,* who was sold as a yearling for only $700 and returned $350,000 as a stakes winner to his owner—a profit of five thousand per cent.

The sales held at the Keeneland racecourse are more than a simple auction. They evoke visions of a theater-in-the-round, a circus, and a prize ring. The auction shed at Keeneland is a spacious amphitheater in which the focus is a square of green sawdust surrounded by a white silk rope, which creates the effect of an effete prize ring. Seats slope upward on three sides. Facing the sawdust square, seated on high stools, are the auctioneers and their assistants. To the layman they look like judges on the bench at night court. On either side of the auctioneers' stand are double, sliding mahogany doors with highly polished brass fittings. On the right side is a long corridor where grooms are giving their yearlings a last-minute brushdown while buyers take one last, long expensive look. At a signal from the auctioneer, a yearling is led into a spotlight by a distinguished, white-coated Negro groom. On the horse's shimmering hip is a number corresponding to a number in the sales catalogue which each prospective buyer has perused carefully. The number appears again over the auctioneer's platform. As the yearling is led around, the auctioneer gives a quick summary of his pedigree and the racing record of his immediate forebears. He then goes after the bids.

The audience consists of the social elite of racing and breeding and their agents. These buyers represent not only American racing stables and breeding farms located in most sections of the United States; some even come from Europe and Australia.

It is more than a conventional auction. It is something like the meeting of a religious cult. The spotlights beat down on the beautiful sacrifice while the auctioneer drones on in a hypnotic chant. Actually the auctioneer is saying: "I've got a two atwoatwoatwoatwoa, I've got a three athreeathreeathreeathreea, fourafourafourafoura, who'll make it a fiveafiveafiveafivea?" While the auctioneer chants, the flick of a finger or the raise of an eyebrow means another thousand-dollar bid from one of the alert buyers in the audience. Along the aisles several sharp-eyed assistants watch for bid signals. Suddenly the auctioneer finds that he's not getting as much as he feels this yearling should bring. He comes to a sudden stop. His voice, like the crack of a whip, startles the colt and alerts the audience: "Now *listen* to me, not enough of you out there payin' attention. This is a mighty fine colt—we gotta get movin'. Fortyeightafortyeighta, fortyeighta, fortynineafortyninea, who'll bid fifty and *close* the gate? O.K., sir, he's yours for $50,000."

Blue Grass youngsters examine every strange object. Here they taste a jeep.

Like a bird in flight, a yearling streaks across the Blue Grass meadow.

Scratching head with hoof,
yearling ignores camera:
others eye strange object.

44

Scratching against tree, youngster cools off in shade on hot Kentucky afternoon.

45

Hoof trimming and shoe fitting are everyday horse-farm chores.

The auctioneer knows about what each yearling should bring and he tries to push his buyers at least that far. Occasionally, in an aside, he becomes pleasantly insulting, "I hope to hell she runs faster than you gentlemen are bidding." Or again, "Hey there, you all better wake up. This one looks just like his daddy." Or, "Now, let's pay attention, gentlemen. This is a *Nashua* colt. Let's study our lessons here."

To relieve the tension when the bidding gets high and the auctioneer wants to keep pushing, he may remark, as the dean of horse auctioneers, George Swinebroad, said at a recent sale, "Gentlemen, only forty thousand bid. Why this colt's dam, if bred to a jackass, would throw the runningest mule ever to come down the pike. Looky here, men, give me another bid." The rapidity with which the auctioneer speaks sounds like the familiar tobacco auctioneer's chants. It takes an expert to determine who is bidding and how the bidding is going.

Although the auctioneer has the speaking part, it is the yearlings that are the stars of the production. They may occasionally mess up the artificial green turf but they behave extraordinarily well. They are slowly walked around the ring, stopped, turned around. The promenade is continued with an occasional posing until the bidding is over. Then the yearling is lead out through the door on the left side as a new prospect makes his entrance from the right. At the auction the buyers make every effort to consider the conformation of the horse, his immediate sire and dam and their racing records. However, all prospective purchasers are swayed almost beyond their control by the appearance of the yearling in the ring, and many a high-priced colt has been purchased almost on his appearance alone.

Now let's get back to the yearlings that did not go to market but are being "broken" and trained for racing. Our yearling is at the point of being led around the stall with surcingle and pad. The next step in his education is called "belly-

46

Eyes wide with terror, yearling trembles as boy "sits him" for the first time.

busting," which is not nearly so harsh as it sounds. A lightweight farm youngster, who has been reared around horses and has been chosen as the yearling's exercise boy, lies gently on his stomach across the yearling's back while the groom holds his halter. Then for the next few days the groom will lead the horse around while the exercise boy quietly and gently rests his weight across his back. After two to four days in this position, the boy inches one leg over and cautiously pulls himself up to a sitting position. Meanwhile the groom continues to lead the horse around the stall until he gets used to the shifting of the boy's weight. Now the exercise boy moves his legs along the sides of the horse to familiarize him with the feel of stirrups.

Next, the horse, with the boy on his back, is led out of doors. After he becomes thoroughly familiar with the boy on his back, he learns to take the bit in his mouth. Care is taken that the yearling's mouth, which is often quite tender, is not injured at this time. After walking outdoors for a few minutes a day, the exercise boy will urge the yearling into a trot while the groom jogs alongside holding the shank, a strap leading to the halter. It is important that the yearling be kept going in one direction and not be allowed to develop bad habits, such as walking backward or shying sideways. After two or three weeks, or until he is completely bridlewise, the horse is ready to be taken out with other yearlings to the training track.

47

On the training track he learns to get along with other horses, to avoid bumping against them, and to run in his own line. This training is highly specialized and, unless there is a training track on the farm, yearlings are taken to regular race tracks. Every morning the "back" track at Keeneland, the horsemen's track in the Blue Grass country, is busy with yearlings and their trainers. The soft early morning sun filters through the fog from 5 to 9 A. M. as the frisky youngsters learn their lessons. Technically this is called training. Schooling, the last stage in a yearling's education, teaches him how to enter and "break" properly from the starting gate.

Now our yearling has become a trained athlete. He is almost two years old, actually not quite that because he was probably born in March or April and became a year old in January. He may weigh in the neighborhood of a thousand pounds. His back is strong enough to hold a jockey and he has been trained to run with different exercise boys on his back so that he will not object to a strange jockey up when he starts racing. Now the trainer is looking him over, checking his "way of going," his attitude, and his physical appearance. Some yearlings mature much faster than others; some must be taken along slowly in "breaking," training, and schooling; some go along very fast. As the famous jockey Eddie Arcaro once said, "Horses are like people. Everybody doesn't have the same aggressiveness or the ambition to knock himself out to make a success. Most horses will dog it and goof off if you let them get away with it."

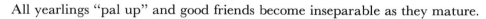

All yearlings "pal up" and good friends become inseparable as they mature.

Morning fog almost obscures horses in dawn workout. Track litter is of previous day.

Racing in the Blue Grass

IF YOU FOLLOW the white fences out the Versailles Pike (U. S. 60 west) from Lexington, you will come upon the horsemen's own track, Keeneland. This is the racing capital of the Blue Grass region. Massive limestone gateposts form the entrance and a wide expanse of lawn, dotted with pin oaks, leads to the distinctive Gothic Revival building that houses offices, promenade, and library.

Like Newmarket, which was built as a private track for King James I, Keeneland was also built originally for a king, for Blue Grass king John Oliver Keene. He conceived and constructed it as a personal racecourse for the sport and entertainment of himself and his friends.

On the "backstretch" at Keeneland. Scene suggests Irish countryside.

Even today, a race meet at Keeneland is still like attending a private gathering. There are no blaring loudspeakers (the management says people come to see races, not hear them). No hot-dog stands are on the lawn, no pitchmen loudly sell souvenirs. Over your shoulder is the hospitable shadow of Jack Oliver Keene acting as host, although his place is now taken by the Blue Grass horse breeders who operate the track as a non-profit venture.

Other great Blue Grass characters have had their own private courses, but Keene's was the biggest. After an extravagant career, which is recounted in another chapter, Jack Keene determined to construct his own racecourse complete with an indoor training track, spacious limestone stalls for horses, and apartments in a main building for his friends and their families. The site was a level spot on his old family estate, perhaps the most ancient land-grant area in the region. For the land on which Keene built was part of an eight thousand-acre tract which had been deeded to his ancestor Francis Keen (Jack Oliver said the *e* was added because the name was too short). It was Patrick Henry, a kinsman, who granted the land at the close of the eighteenth century. He was then governor of Virginia.

Keene had a royal imagination. He visualized a palace for horses and, incidentally, for people. He designed it himself and each year poured more money into the grounds and the lovingly constructed stone castle. When the building was almost completed, the stalls and indoor track finished, Keene's money ran out. Asked what he planned to do next he said, "I've spent so much money on it no

Ben Jones, famous Calumet trainer, is out in early morning on the Keeneland track.

one will be able to afford to buy it." He was wrong. The thoroughbred breeders of the Blue Grass got together and in 1935 worked out a co-operative plan to buy the property and finish the work so well advanced by Jack Keene. In October 1936 the gates were opened and Kentucky's thoroughbreds had their own track.

Most of the horses running at Keeneland are foaled and broken in the neighborhood and trained and schooled on the model five-eighths-mile training track located back of the main one-and-one-sixteenth-mile course. There in the early morning sun many of the great men in racing may be seen overseeing the training and schooling of great horses. Ben Jones, the training genius of Calumet, and a consistent Derby winner, used to ride a mule at these workouts. He now rides a distinctive white pony.

Long shadows of the early sun make grotesque images of horses and men. In and around the grandstand the "stoopers" are on hand, men who spend the morning stooping over to examine thrown-away tickets of the previous day's races, hoping they will find an uncashed ticket dropped by a careless bettor. When caught in this odd position, they are ejected.

The early morning hours at Keeneland are the height of the day for owners, trainers, exercise boys, and horses. Maidens (colts and fillies who have not yet won their first race) will be learning to break from the starting gate. The racer should be out of the gate in one long leap, say the trainers, faster than a car when the light changes and before the car behind can sound its horn. Other young hopefuls

51

Bettors swarm over attractive outdoor paddock during the Keeneland spring meet.

Handsome two-year-old poses in winners' "circle."

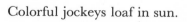

Colorful jockeys loaf in sun.

These gates, with bronze horse figures on the pillars, lead from paddock to track.

will be galloping or breezing, a brisk running gait between galloping and driving. When breezing, the horse is given his head and allowed to go as fast, within reason, as he wishes.

Meanwhile the entire backstretch will be humming. Almost any day five hundred to seven hundred horses and all the personnel needed to school, train, and care for them will headquarter in the backstretch. There the kitchen staff prepares twelve hundred meals three times a day for hungry track workers. But by nine o'clock in the morning, when most of the world is getting to work, the horses and their attendants will be through for the day. Before 11 A. M. the training track is deserted.

When a meet is in progress, and there are two a year, Keeneland will be active on many levels all day. By the time the horses have left the training track the car hustlers who park your car will have arrived. Before twelve o'clock, patrons are being directed to parking spaces by these men. There is no charge for parking at Keeneland, but the hustlers expect twenty-five cents to one dollar, depending on the spot you are ushered into. The men are polite and efficient, but always save a few spaces near the entrance for latecoming big tippers. By one-thirty the well-dressed crowd is parked and pouring through the gates to the clubhouse and grandstand.

Keeneland is unique in that it has no free list. Everyone pays, except owners, and trainers. Admission gates are located just inside the "Castle Gates."

A long stone corridor extends past the stairway which leads to the racing library. This distinctive collection of horse lore contains priceless racing publications of the past as well as current photographs and records.

On the left is the clubroom, which houses elaborate racing trophies. This spacious room was a favorite of Jack Oliver Keene's. He believed in large open fireplaces and built one for giants in this room. It takes a log six feet long and three feet in diameter. On the right of the clubroom is a line of stall-type doors with brass fittings. Behind them are the offices of the Keeneland Racing Association.

The end of the long corridor discloses a charming vista encompassing two hundred and ten acres devoted to thoroughbred racing. The abundant grass grows even where thousands of racing fans trample it. The clubhouse, on the left, is already filled with affable owners and trainers, and their guests—the elite of Blue Grass society. Stretching out in front is the broad lawn, bright with native dogwood, redbud, and spirea. Directly in front is the grandstand with one hundred forty boxes, each seating six patrons. The best seats for viewing the races, however, are the five thousand unreserved seats in the grandstand.

A country-fair atmosphere prevails. Sportsmen stroll from the grandstand to clubhouse and over to the open-paddock area, under the shade trees, where the racers are readied for the track. Owners and trainers prepare their horses within the open arena that Keene planned as his training track. Before each race there is an exodus from grandstand and clubhouse to the open paddock. Interested bettors have a last good look at their favorites. According to the experts, it is a good place to spot potential winners.

When Roscoe Goose, old-time trainer, looks them over he advises, "Be sure your horse seems bright and cheerful and makes a good appearance. Some horses like to run and go like water running downhill. Others sulk and whipping makes them worse; so watch for the sulky look and the pinned-back ears. There are a lot of loafers too, horses who will not give out with what they've got."

Miss Virginia Hayes, librarian at the Lexington Public Library and daughter of a distinguished owner-trainer, says, "I watch for the look in the eye of the trainer

Shy and superstitious jockey ducks his head, thinking photo may bring bad luck.

as he gives the boy his last-minute instructions. If he has a hopeful gleam I think his horse has a good chance." They also tell the story of the two experts who were losing heavily but noticed that the two old ladies standing nearby had cashed tickets every race. Finally one of the gentlemen stepped over and said, "You ladies seem to be doing pretty well, would you mind letting us in on your system?" "Oh, we have lots of systems," the eldest replied. "Today we're betting on the horses with the longest tails."

Membership in the Keeneland clubhouse is strictly limited to the horse fraternity—men and women actively engaged in raising or racing thoroughbreds. There are some four hundred fifty members. Spouses are permitted, as well as children. No one can buy his way into the Keeneland clubhouse; it is for members only, and their guests. This does not mean that they have the best view of the races or even the most comfortable spot from which to view them. The veranda of the clubhouse gets the direct sun about eye level from 2 to 4 P. M. Furthermore, it is located so far from the finish line that it is impossible to tell the results until the winning numbers go up on the giant electric board.

The one great advantage of being a clubhouse member is the privilege of patronizing the bar and restaurant presided over by headwaiter "Kentucky Gus" Petty. Gus, an elderly gentleman of color, has been at Keeneland since its

55

opening, and before that he spent many years at the old Kentucky Association track in Lexington. He knows the tastes and foibles of most of the old-timers and serves them handily.

"Some of my customers," says Gus, "will sit around and chew the races over for two or three hours after they're finished. I've had them stay 'til nine o'clock, and I've had some of them sign checks for $1,000 too. You've got to be a big man to do that."

Gus explained that many of the "regulars" reserve tables every day of the meet. "I always have a couple of tables for Mr. Leslie Combs and for Mr. Hancock and Mrs. Helen Carruthers," he confided. Gus gets "pretty good tips" on the race horses from their owners, but, he says, "You can't depend on it because they don't know who's going to win either; they're just hoping."

A true race-track philosopher, Gus continues, "You just can't beat them but you can live off them if you know what you're doing. The racing game is a lot different from what it used to be. They check on everything and everybody nowadays. But if they had run all the old-timers off the track that were doing wrong in the old days, there wouldn't have been anybody there at all."

Gus is right. Things have changed since the "good old days," and the most important changes resulted from introduction of the Film Patrol. Before races were photographed on motion-picture film, from start to finish, many jockeys got away with, if not murder, at least mayhem. As one of the old-time jockeys put it, "You win any way you can and you do whatever you can get away with." Those were the days of slashing at the competing jockey with the whip, putting on a leg lock to keep a rival from passing, or crowding a horse into the rail.

Such tactics rarely occur now. Jockeys, trainers, and owners know it will show up in detail on the film. This means the horse may be disqualified and the jockey grounded.

Modern motion-picture cameras with telephoto lenses follow the race action all the way around the track. This equipment is housed in two tall but inconspicuous towers at Keeneland. A station wagon races after the running horses, picking up the film from the towers and rushing it back for developing and viewing.

At first the Film Patrol was suspect. Now everyone approves of it. Owners and trainers see how their horses are performing and often are able to correct bad running habits. Jockeys no longer worry about being blamed for wrongs they do not commit. Filming the races has another important effect. Jockeys are more confident. In the old days, if a legitimate opening showed up in a potentially dangerous spot, the jockey, knowing he might get jammed into the rail or purposely jostled by another horse, would think twice before riding through. Now he knows he is safe from intentional fouls because the Film Patrol has taken most of the rough riding out of racing.

Other old-time chicanery and flim-flam have also disappeared. Even the meanings of some old-time racing expressions are fast being lost. "Getting his goat" once referred to the stealing of the stable mascot of a racer to throw him off his feed and so decrease his chances of winning. Thoroughbreds, like many sensitive

The Old Keen Place next to the Keeneland racecourse once entertained Lafayette.

Trainers and owners give their jockeys the last word before mounting for the race.

Horses are saddled outdoors at Keeneland racecourse by their own trainers or owners.

Young "railbirds" in early morning watch a two-year-old "breeze" around the track.

and high-strung people, hate being alone. They become permanently attached to a stable pet or mascot. The most popular of these are ponies, goats, chickens, and dogs and cats. Some years ago, "Peanuts," the pony mascot of the fleet gelding *Exterminator,* died suddenly. The great race horse refused all food for two days. In desperation, his owners placed the remains of the pony in the stall with him to prove to him the pony was indeed dead. All night, the stable boys say, the gelding lay with his head over the body. By morning he was convinced that "Peanuts" was dead. Later that day he began to eat again. He lived on for many years with a new pony as his companion.

Phrases like "dark horse," "ringer," or "horse of another color" have ceased to have their original race-track connotation. There is no point in painting a horse or changing his spots now that all major tracks require the official Jockey Club registration number to be permanently tattooed on the upper lip of the horse. A new photographic "fingerprint" system is now being used on most tracks. The growth on the inside of the horse's lower leg (called a chestnut or night eye) is photographed, measured, and classified. What the lip tattoo and the new photo system did to eliminate ringers, the saliva test, now required of all winning horses, has done to eliminate the onetime practice of doping horses to make them run faster.

61

Not only the ethics but also the sport itself has changed in Kentucky. Racing at Keeneland has come a long way from the October day in 1793 when the trustees of the village of Lexington decided that "horse racing in the streets is hereafter prohibited as being too dangerous to the citizens; but it is authorized at the west end of the Commons where stud horses are shown."

A few years after this a small group of Kentucky settlers met at Postlethwaite's Tavern (later to become the famous Phoenix Hotel) and planned the first track. It was located on the present land of the Lexington Cemetery. The next group formed to promote racing was the Lexington Jockey Club, which numbered Henry Clay, then at the peak of his career, among its charter members.

Kentucky's longest-lived racecourse started in 1826. It furnished sport for more than one hundred years. This was the beginning of "Chittlin' Switch," as the old Kentucky Association track became affectionately known throughout the racing world. A "chittlin'," or chitterling, as the dictionary would have it, is the very edible small intestine of the pig. It has been a delicacy among Kentucky's Negro population for generations. But it is also considered mighty good eating by most white trainers, jockeys, and owners. The word "switch" relates to the railroad switch at the point where the horses were shipped into the track.

There is a story about the southern jockey who was showing a northern boy around one day and suggested that they go and have some chitterlings. "Never heard of it, what is it?" said the northern boy. The southerner assured him it was just about the best eating in the entire world. The northerner was unconvinced. "I'll bet you $10.00 it is not as good as porterhouse steak," he ventured. "I'll take that bet," replied the southerner. "Let's ask Clifford Porter, the jockey trainer, to decide." They cornered Porter, told him about the bet, and asked him to declare the winner. "Well, I couldn't rightly judge that," he said. "I never have tasted porterhouse steak."

Unlike Keeneland today, there was no clubhouse when the old Kentucky Association track was opened. The judge's stand was actually part of the cowpens. It was a track where country fairs, cattle and stallion shows were held. The organization was officially called the Kentucky Association for the Improvement of Breeds of Livestock. There was no charge to get into the grounds, which were originally unfenced. The grandstand fee was twenty-five cents. Few women attended, and betting was a man-to-man business. These were the days of long races and of three-mile heats. In 1835 three horses, *Sarah Miller, Jim Allen,* and *Greyfoot* participated in a great sixteen-mile race. The old-timers say that thoroughbreds run a lot faster today, but that the bottoms have been bred out of them.

Racing prospered in the Blue Grass. Not even the grim days of the Civil War dampened the enthusiasm of Kentucky's horse lovers. Stallion shows were held and dash races were introduced. Everyone backed the horse from his own community. In 1876, on the fiftieth anniversary of the track, a great match race was run between *Aristides,* who had won the first Kentucky Derby the year before, and the celebrated racer *Ten Broeck.* It was a fine day and a fine race, but it is said that Woodford County, home of *Ten Broeck,* went bankrupt when he lost. A few years

At fall meet, horses appear for last race. Most of crowd is still at paddock.

Groom leads racer for outdoor saddling. Bad-weather saddling area is in background.

His race over, thoroughbred is "cooled out" by his handlers in the "backstretch."

later, in 1889, there was a different kind of disaster during the centennial of organized racing in Kentucky. The rain came down in torrents, which bothered no one unduly until the clubhouse leaked so badly that water got into the whiskey. Only then was there great consternation among the celebrants.

So racing went on at "Chittlin' Switch" through the turn of the century, which brought the day of the great gamblers. Then began the days of elaborate parties; women began to put in an appearance at the track. The silk purse which hung at the finish line to be collected by the winner was undoubtedly a woman's idea. It was women, too, who brought style and emphasis on fashionable attire to the track.

The old Kentucky Association lasted until 1932 when it held its last spring meet. For a short time racing languished in the home of the thoroughbred. Then the breeders of the Blue Grass country took over and, using the solid foundation laid by Jack Oliver Keene, they built the horsemen's own track, Keeneland.

Colorful tulips, bright spring garments, light up Churchill Downs on Derby Day.

The Kentucky Derby

THE RECORD does not show any Blue Grass horse owner selling his soul to the Devil in the fashion of Faust and other fictional characters. But this is only because not even the Devil can guarantee a Kentucky Derby winner in return. For winning this great horse race is the ultimate goal of the thoroughbred breeder. Harry Payne Whitney put the ecstasy of it into words when his filly *Regret* finished two lengths ahead in the forty-first running of the Kentucky Derby in 1915. "I don't care if she never wins another race or if she never starts in another race. She has won the greatest race in America and I am satisfied."

The Kentucky classic is traditionally held on the first Saturday in May at the Churchill Downs racecourse. It is for three-year-old thoroughbreds only. Each one carries 126 pounds, which includes the jockey. The length of the race is one and one quarter miles. Finishing first means winning well over $100,000, plus a $5,000 gold cup. But it is the deathless honor and glory that hold the greatest value for the Blue Grass horseman.

The Derby is not held in the inner Blue Grass region but on the outskirts of the cosmopolitan city of Louisville in what is sometimes called the outer Blue Grass or Bear Grass country. Louisville, though seventy-five miles from Lexington, nevertheless has a dedicated population of equine aficionados. A group of sixty-five otherwise ruggedly individualistic businessmen of the city recently became horse owners by purchasing co-operatively a well-bred race horse. They prudently named it *Go for Broke*.

In the inner Blue Grass, Derby preparations on some horse farms start years before the actual race. Potential winners are observed minutely shortly after they have been foaled. Running space in the big race is limited, and the competition to be accepted is rougher, and more scientific, than being admitted into any Ivy League college.

By Derby-time each year, over a hundred three-year-olds are nominated, that is made eligible to start in the race. However, the biggest Derby field ever to start was twenty-two in 1928.

But the Derby is more than a horse race. It is, for the Blue Grass country, the social event of the year. Thousands of communications go out to friends and relatives, acquaintances and business contacts, inviting them to stay over. Thirty house guests are by no means unusual.

Festivities begin two weeks before the great event with the running of the Blue Grass Stakes, an important Derby trial run. On Derby Day the exodus from the Blue Grass begins at dawn. The trip is made by car and by plane, though it is only a twenty-minute flight from Blue Grass Field to Louisville.

But the most luxurious way of making the trip to Churchill Downs is on Greyhound Scenicruiser buses which some hosts charter for their guests. The Derby Day party gets going on the bus, which is equipped with bar, bartender, and a sumptuous supply of southern snacks to be nibbled along the way. Outside Louisville, at Cherokee Park, the Scenicruisers stop for a pre-Derby picnic brunch. Mrs. Leslie Combs provides for about forty in her Derby Day bus party. Her lunch baskets are filled with fried chicken, Kentucky ham, homemade beaten biscuits, deviled eggs, cheese sandwiches, and homemade brownies baked by Mrs. Combs' cook. From ten to twelve o'clock in the morning of Derby Day, Cherokee Park is a happy picnic ground. The atmosphere is particularly festive around the buses that produce well-chilled silver julep goblets for that delicious traditional southern drink.

Festivities culminate in the post-Derby parties held on Sunday after the running of the big race. By far the biggest is the outdoor spread extended to some four hundred invited guests by Mr. and Mrs. Leslie Combs at their Spendthrift estate. This party started as an intimate gathering of forty or fifty Blue Grass friends.

"So many people kept phoning," Mrs. Combs explains, "and asking if it would be all right to bring their house guests along that it got too big and we had to limit the number by sending written invitations."

Because of the traditional hospitality of the Blue Grass region, this move brought complications and even competitive parties. The Combs party, however, remains the climax which closes the Derby season. Mrs. Combs' biggest problem, as the party got bigger, was the threat of rain. "How could I possibly have four hundred people in the house?" she asks. "But my husband, Leslie, came to the rescue. He had a tent put up and now, rain or shine, we have our Kentucky Derby party."

Small tables dot the lawn under the great tent and ten waiters move about serving hot cheese croquettes, turkey in aspic, creamed peas with mushrooms, beaten biscuits, garlic toast squares, and finally, fresh strawberry sherbet. "The strawberry sherbet is a great favorite," Mrs. Combs remarks. "It is probably good for the Derby Day hangover."

Many of the Derby Day hangovers start with the Derby eve parties given throughout the region. In Louisville there are always gatherings at the Brown and Seelback hotels, as well as in the homes of prominent citizens. Dance bands are imported and the atmosphere is a combination of Mardi Gras eve in New Orleans and New Year's Eve in almost any city in the world.

Louisville is bursting with people who have suddenly become horse experts. Apartments that would normally rent for $200 a month bring $200 for Derby week-end. Local citizens move out of their apartments into quarters with relatives to pick up extra money. Hotel rooms are at a very high premium. Some years ago Colonel Phil Chinn, a famous Blue Grass horse trader, arrived in Louisville the day before the Derby. He applied for accommodation to the room clerk of the Brown Hotel and was told there was no room. The Colonel asked to speak to the manager, then somewhat new to his job. After talking to the manager for some time and impressing him with his importance, Colonel Chinn asked whether or not a room was going to be made available. The manager decided not to make this important decision himself and got the hotel's owner on the telephone. After a short conversation, the owner said to the manager, "Is Colonel Chinn still there?" "Yes, he is," said the manager. "Well by all means let him have the room," said the hotel owner, "for if he stays there fifteen more minutes, he will talk you out of an entire floor."

Pedigreed two-year-olds are led by handlers in pre-Derby showing.

Drum majorettes, U. S. Army Band stand at attention for pre-Derby showing.

Leaving the paddock, jockey guides thoroughbred under clubhouse extension toward track.

On the big day, traffic moves solidly all morning out to Churchill Downs. There, extra police have been put on. Louisville has an efficient corps of women police who join with the men to control the record crowds.

Outside the admission gates, banners fly and pitchmen hawk souvenirs. Few patrons stop. Intent on getting inside, they swarm through the wide columns. Just inside the main entrance is an underpass that leads to the spacious infield. This is the goal of those fans without grandstand seats. On the well-manicured grass they set up their beachhead for the day. These dedicated Derby lovers carry lunch baskets, camp stools, shooting sticks, beach towels, umbrellas, and enough bourbon to stock the bars of a fair-sized city. Out in this sunny, circular pasture some sixty thousand fans spread out to spend a pleasant and exciting afternoon.

Within the sprawling building of Churchill Downs is a baffling maze of passages, escalators, stairways, private elevators, restaurants, and bars. It is said that only Brownie Leach, the saturnine publicity director, knows where all the secret rooms and hidden booths, coves, niches, suites, offices, salons, and saloons are located. Among the sequestered spots is the six-room private apartment of Churchill Downs' president, reachable by private elevator. Room number 21 is an ultra-private sanctum that accommodates over a hundred guests and has its

Final parade before post time of Derby finds photographers ready on the track.

Derby costumes cover a wide range from fashionable to fantastic. Girl's skintights are unusual.

own balcony with a fine view of the finish line. It has its private buffet and bar service as well.

Other screened areas rarely seen by the casual eye of the public are the Directors' Room, where visiting celebrities are greeted, and the Matt Winn room, named for the man mainly responsible for making the Derby a national institution. In the latter, admission is by card only and less than a hundred such cards are issued. Members of the press, some 225 top turf scribes, have a well-placed vantage spot on the fourth tier of the building. Press quarters are served by a small and always overcrowded elevator named for the late Buck Weaver of the Louisville *Times*. The rooftop is the private preserve of photographers who come from all over the world. Some cameramen arrive early in the morning to set up and focus on the finish line from what they consider the best angle. One magazine shipped hundreds of pounds of equipment, employed a heart specialist, and hooked up a portable electrocardiograph instrument to a woman who had made a sizable wager on *Silky Sullivan*, the California in-and-outer. Unfortunately, *Silky* showed no class in the Derby and the heart action of the bettor proved to be wholly uninteresting.

Directly over the finish line is the photofinish camera booth, and directly next to it the two TV announcers enjoy an unobstructed view. Topping the whole pyramid of workers, bettors, celebrities, Kentucky colonels, grandes dames, and dolls and their guys, are the TV cameramen who work from a shedlike roof over the main section of the press box.

In the grandstand or clubhouse, it is possible to eat well, even on Derby Day. Dining room A seats six hundred but has no visibility. Dining room B, where four hundred can be accommodated, offers a view of the track. The central area of the building includes the enclosed paddock where the Derby runners may be viewed. From the paddock the horses saunter through the mid-section of the building onto the track.

An occasion not to be missed. Some racing fans attend in wheel chairs.

There are lots of escalators, but the one leading up to the Paddock Bar gets the most use. Derby Day is also Mint Julep Day in Kentucky. In addition to the thousands of juleps served in the bars, they are also concocted with machinelike precision (and machinelike taste) and sold throughout the grandstand area. Souvenir Kentucky Derby julep cups and glasses are available at stands on the grounds.

Everyone wants to bet on the Derby and everyone is given every opportunity. Special windows are open for Derby bets and before the big race any one of the 424 selling windows will take your money and give you a pari-mutuel ticket.

It is probable that not a lot of money has been won in the Kentucky Derby in recent years. Certainly there has been no upset like that of the 1913 race when jockey Roscoe Goose booted home the long shot *Donerail* to pay the biggest odds

Between races baton twirler performs while army band plays. On next page is infield on Derby Day.

Everybody bets on Derby Day. Some win, too.

ever: $91.45 to one dollar. The race now is usually won by a favorite or near favorite. A few of the big racing farms, like Lucille and Gene Markey's Calumet, have won the Derby seven times. Closest to this record is Colonel E. R. Bradley with four winners. The same trainers, Ben Jones for Calumet and H. J. Thompson for Bradley, also take pride in these victories.

Fastest of all the horses over the present course was Calumet's *Whirlaway,* who covered the distance in two minutes, one and two fifths seconds. The slowest winner was *Stone Street,* who took thirteen and four fifths seconds longer on a heavy, muddy track.

As proof that good sires get good offspring, it should be noted that eight Derby winners sired Derby winners. In the case of *Reigh Count* there was a triple winning streak. *Reigh Count,* who won the 1928 Derby, sired *Count Fleet,* the 1943 winner, who in turn sired *Count Turf,* who won in 1951. There is another three generation succession. *Pensive,* who won in 1944, sired *Ponder,* who won in 1949. *Ponder* sired *Needles,* the 1956 winner.

Jockeys have also piled up multiple wins. Most consistent winner has been Eddie Arcaro, who has scored five times beginning in 1938 with *Lawrin.* When asked how it feels to ride so many Derby winners, Arcaro replied, "Not so good. Just think how many I've lost." (He has ridden in twenty so far and is still going strong.) The only jockeys to win two Derbies in succession were both Negroes. Isaac Murphy, considered by many old-timers the greatest of them all, won the 1890 and 1891 Derbies after winning the 1884 event. Jimmie Winkfield won in 1901 and 1902.

Jockeys have been responsible for some of the most exciting moments as their mounts neared the finish line. In 1933 *Brokers Tip* and *Headplay* were neck and neck in the stretch when jockeys Meade and Fisher fought a pitched battle for the lead,

74

using their whips on each other rather than on their horses. In 1957, with *Gallant Man* taking the lead over *Iron Liege*, Jockey Willie Shoemaker misjudged the finish and, thinking he had won, stood up in the stirrups. This threw *Gallant Man* off-stride. In the one one-hundredth of a second, *Iron Liege*, well ridden by Willie Hartack, took over and won by a nose.

But perhaps the most unusual of all jockey misadventures occurred back in 1926. In the early part of the race, jockey Kurtsinger, racing along the inside rail, suddenly saw one of the spectators lean far out. The jockey ducked but the fan grabbed his whip as he flew by. This so unnerved him that he finished seventh.

This type of occurrence can never happen again. The infield spectators are now well separated from the rail. In the early days, fans often had to be cleared from the track before the race could begin.

The first Kentucky Derby was held on May 17, 1875. It got its name from the race in England at Epsom Downs. The English Derby was founded in 1780 and named for the twelfth Earl of Derby. The earl has been quoted as saying, "The race is called a Darby, the hat is called a bowler." Be that as it may, in the United States the correct pronunciation of the Kentucky classic is "derby" and the hat goes by the same name. The first Derby was won easily by *Aristides*, who raced against the best available competition of the day.

This race was held at the Louisville Association track, but the grounds were originally owned by the Churchill family, and the appellation, Churchill Downs, was later given by a newspaperman back in the days when the Derby was young.

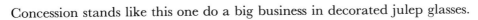

Concession stands like this one do a big business in decorated julep glasses.

Horse fan tries to get some information from jockeys as they wait between races.

Today the whole nation attends the Derby. Television carries it into every farm and city. The "A" wire of the Associated Press has never been broken into, once the words, "The horses are on the track for the Kentucky Derby," are spoken.

It is a matchless spectacle. The sleek horses prance in review. Five massed bands break into the tear-jerking strains of "My Old Kentucky Home" and a lump wells up in every throat, including the throats of those visitors who have never previously traveled further south than Southport, Connecticut, or Southampton, Long Island. Seventy-five years of sentiment and tradition congeal in this moment. The horses, stepping high, begin their leisurely parade past the grandstand and to the starting post.

During this interval, last-minute bets are laid, bands are marching and playing, champion drum majorettes dance and toss their batons high in the air. But nothing interferes with the concentration on the horses now approaching the starting gate.

Newsmen, TV cameramen, motion picture and magazine photographers cluster on the clubhouse roof.

After a few seconds' jockeying, the thoroughbreds are locked into the starting gate, the starting button is pushed, the bell rings, and a hundred thousand voices thunder, "THEY'RE OFF!"

Then follow the fastest two and a fraction minutes in the sporting world. The thoroughbreds fly by the grandstand, still bunched, and all the great winners of the past seem to be running with them—*Black Gold, Swaps, Ben Brush, Exterminator, Pensive, Whirlaway, Old Rosebud, Flying Ebony, Citation, Twenty Grand, Gallahadion, Zev,* and *Gallant Fox* matching stride for stride.

The horses seem to be gliding by on the far side of the track. Then miraculously they are heading into the homestretch. The air is alive with exhilaration and tension. Human hearts and horses' hoofs pound in unison as they drive to the finish line. Another running of the Kentucky Derby is over. The crowd slowly unwinds.

After one Derby, two stable boys who had bet on the wrong horse were discussing the future. "What are you going to do now?" asked one boy. "I'm going down to the river," he said. "What about you?" "Well, I'll go down to the river with you, boy" he answered, "but I'm coming back!"

This is *Bulldog,* head of a great line of runners, shortly before he died.

The Stallions

THE REAL ARISTOCRACY of the Blue Grass region are the successful sires. These top-money racing stallions, after a short but triumphant career on the tracks, return to their birthplace, there to become the fathers of tomorrow's fleet stakes winners.

Their success will depend upon many people as well as a variety of unpredictable circumstances. The breeding of top racing thoroughbreds has many of the elements of gambling.

Regardless of the various complications involved in the career of a successful blue-blooded sire, he will lead anything but a dog's life. His earning power will be even greater than it was when he was racing. Should his get be winners on the race tracks, he will be pampered, admired, insured, idolized, and ultimately venerated. Huge crowds of tourists arriving by Cadillac, jeep, and bus will stand in awe of him. Parents will take unnecessary chances by crowding close to the white fences and allowing their children to get within harm's way of these temperamental thoroughbreds.

But let us begin the story of his retirement at the end of his racing career. Most of the popular racing stallions are retired to stud after two to four winning

Nasrullah, great sire of thoroughbred champions, rears up on way to breeding shed.

years on the track. They are then four or five years old. The announcement that a *Swaps, Gallant Man,* or a *Nashua* is being retired to stud is big news and creates more stir in the horse world than the retirement of a major corporation executive in the business world. The most important years of the stallion's life are still before him.

Among the factors that will influence the stallion's success as a sire is his money-earning ability while racing. *Nashua,* who had a short track career, earned $1,288,565 in exactly thirty races. Each race lasted an average of 1 minute 47⅘ seconds, which means that during his actual working hours he earned $23,906.58 per minute. It is assumed, often erroneously, that stallions are able to pass along their speedy qualities to their progeny. This is sometimes true. But it is also true that a success at stud will depend upon his previous pedigree, the bloodlines that have combined to make him great. It will depend to an even higher degree upon the mares to which he is bred.

Our stallion has been a winner. Upon retirement he is loaded into a private car or a plush horse van to be shipped back home to the Blue Grass country where he was born. Every possible precaution is taken to see that he gets home safely. Stallions retiring to stud in the Blue Grass travel not only by private car or van but are often flown in from racecourses all over the world. They land at Blue Grass Field, located just a few furlongs from Keeneland racecourse on the edge of the city of Lexington. Most such journeys are uneventful, but a few years ago a fine Irish stallion, being imported to one of the Blue Grass farms, became overexcited during the flight. Five hundred miles off the Irish coast, he began kicking out the sides of the plane. Because of his frenzied, savage lunging, his grooms were unable to quiet him with a sedative. Imminent danger faced all on board, and reluctantly the pilot made the only possible decision. Twenty thousand feet above the Atlantic he shot and killed the $10,000 stallion.

Stallion transportation is always a delicate operation. As soon as the horse arrives he will be examined carefully by one of the many outstanding veterinarians in the Lexington area. This is important because here is a million dollar investment, and a delicate one. Like most people making a long trip, horses are also subject to draughts. "Shipping fever" is quite common.

His new residence will be one of the four types of Blue Grass farms. Most interesting of these is the full-scale operation of Lucille and Gene Markey, who own Calumet Farm. This romantic and visually rewarding racing-breeding horse farm breeds stallions, rears foals, and trains yearlings on its own racecourse. Calumet's outstanding produce—colts, horses, fillies, and mares—are big-money winners on the tracks of America and Europe. If a stallion has raced under the Calumet colors, he will naturally be retired to stud on that magnificent farm. Equally important, but representing a different kind of operation, is Spendthrift Farm. On this large-scale commercial breeding farm, stallions stand at stud at a price. Outstanding mares are brought to Spendthrift from nearby to be bred. Other brood mares belonging to Spendthrift's owner, Leslie Combs, and his associates, are bred on the farm. Its annual crop of yearlings are offered for sale at the Keeneland auctions.

Handling the mare at breeding time can be hazardous. This one almost got away.

Mare is exposed to "teaser" (stallion not used for breeding) to determine her readiness.

Also outstanding in this field is A. B. "Bull" Hancock's Claiborne Farm near Paris, Kentucky. Other grand-scale commercial horse farms include Elmendorf, Almahurst, Darby Dan, and Mereworth. Visitors to the Blue Grass are awed by the incredible mileage of clean white fences that are repainted every spring. Mereworth Farm is unique because it has the only black fences in the countryside.

Scattered between the larger farms is the third type. This is the small Kentucky farm where horse raising is only a part of the total economic operation of the farm. Tobacco is in many cases the major crop, but no Kentucky farmer who can afford to have a few brood mares and perhaps a stallion or two can stay out of the horse business.

A new development in the Blue Grass operates exclusively with stallions. This is the unique Stallion Station, near Lexington. Here there are no foaling barns, no yearlings, no brood mares. Some fifteen outstanding stallions in residence hold court, while brood mares are brought to them from throughout the Blue Grass area.

Housing for retired stallions is always comfortable by horse, or even human, standards, and usually palatial. Every stall is large and bright with gleaming brass fittings decorating mahogany sliding doors. Walls are rubbed and waxed; some are of rare polished woods. Each stall is fitted with two large iron rings where the stallion can be hitched while being groomed.

Every stallion has a personal groom, a man who corresponds to a valet in human personal affairs. The groom brushes his coat until it is glossy. He cleans out his hoofs and combs his tail and mane. His groom also gives him a thorough physical examination. He wipes out his eyes and sees that his nose is clean. He watches especially for any danger signals. The groom's responsibility extends to noting intestinal disorders and tending them promptly when they occur. Since the groom cannot be on the alert twenty-four hours a day, the recently invented

◀ This is *Citation,* of Calumet Farm; when first let out he romps in paddock.

Neighing *Citation* seems to give horse laugh to viewers.

FOLLOWING PAGE *Nashua,* standing at Spendthrift Farm, is groomed by Tom Harbut, whose father groomed *Man o' War.*

A group of *Nashua's* first foals play around the water trough on Spendthrift Farm.

A group of *Swaps'* (*Nashua's* great rival) foals pose in Blue Grass on Darby Dan Farm.

Maze of fences show individual paddocks at Spendthrift used to keep stallions separated.

Equi-larm has come into limited use. This is a moisture detector which is built into a breastplate that attaches to the horse's chest. The sensitive mechanism transmits the presence of any undue moisture through an electronic receiver to alert the groom or the farm manager. At any sign of stomach upset, usually indicated by fever or excessive perspiration, stallions are kept on their feet and walked slowly around. A twisted intestine, caused by a sick horse thrashing about on a stall floor, means almost certain death.

Most ailments of stallions are not so serious. Stallions sometimes become slightly lame and are prone to colds and minor skin diseases. The whole physical well-being of the stallion is the province of his groom and he checks over his charge with great care each day.

Grooms become very attached to their stallions and take pride in grooming them competitively. A stallion must always look his best on a moment's notice, for one of his owners or a prospective breeder may drop in to look him over. Most stallions enjoy showing-off before spectators. This is fortunate because the great American public, children and adults, all want to see the great horse heroes. Clem Brooks, *Nashua's* groom, says that *Nashua* loves to draw himself up proudly and show off for the onlookers. He is especially pompous and does his best prancing for the crowds of admirers discharged from sight-seeing buses. Every stallion has a distinct personality, and grooms quickly become aware of their temperaments. Clem says of *Nashua* that he is "one horse that don't bluff. If you let him get away with chasing you, he'll run you right out of the country." Tom Harbut, who occasionally handles *Nashua* but is the groom of *Jet Pilot* and *Gallant Man,* says that there are some horses "you just have to challenge or they will bluff you every time." Harbut, whose father was groom to *Man o' War,* has learned that most horses will back down if you show them "who's boss." "You've got to handle him carefully, otherwise he'll get too wild to handle," says Harbut. "It isn't just that the horse is too valuable to let him jump around, it's that I'm too valuable, too."

The stallion's groom supervises the finest of equine cuisine. The best fresh hay is in the racks all the time. Crimped or crushed oats may be treated with wheat germ and natural vitamin B. Most stallions at some time during the year get vitamins and minerals. Diet is extremely important because a stallion is likely to lose as much as two to four hundred pounds during his busy breeding season.

Every groom makes sure that his stallion gets enough exercise. A horse may become lethargic after being retired to stud. If he doesn't exercise himself enough, he is likely to be given enough rope, say thirty to forty feet, and urged to run around in a circle at a trot or a slow gallop. Stallions are very rarely ridden because, once out of the habit of having a boy up regularly, they become hard to handle. Boys who can ride them are rare in the Blue Grass, and expensive. Therefore, one seldom sees a horseman on any of the Blue Grass farms.

While the groom takes care of the stallion's health and daily comforts, his owner or manager is looking after his future by selecting the mares that will become the dams of his foals. His date book for the first season at stud, and indeed for every subsequent season, is critically important. When the stallion's manager is looking over the mares whose owners are willing to pay the necessary fee, he looks for an animal whose qualities will complement those of his horse. Oversimplified, this means that if his stallion is short and sturdy he looks for a long, rangy mare. If the stallion is a fast short-distance runner, he hopes to find a reasonably speedy mare with lots of endurance. All breeding is done to produce faster horses with reasonable endurance, and each foal inherits some of the characteristics of both his dam and sire. Every breeder is attempting to breed out all the deficiencies and to produce a Derby winner.

Other problems enter into the manager's complex booking job. A stallion just starting at stud is unproven. His get are likely to see a race at least once, but the best proven dams are not easy to book, especially when the stallion's service fee may range from $1,000 to $10,000. The manager of the brood mares has an equally difficult problem. There are only a limited number of "popular" stallions. These are the highly publicized horses that everyone wants his mare bred to. When the yearling sales come around, breeders know bids will be higher for their offspring. Too, there is always a chance that his get will be as speedy as he himself was on the racing circuit.

Famous "producer" mare *"Boat"* exercises in pasture. She is daughter of *Man o' War*.

Every owner is as individualistic as his stallion and swears by his own system of selective breeding. Some are very fanciful indeed. Most popular might be called the "fastest-to-fastest" system. The breeder considers the fastest mare and breeds her to the fastest stallion that complements her qualities of conformation. Another system is called "the nick," and the breeder considers the pedigree of the mare and stallion to bring together two proven bloodlines. The stallion may be of the famous *Ben Brush* line; the dam, the *Fair Play* line. It is assumed that because these two lines individually have produced great runners in the past the combination will do so. "Nicks" have often worked out well (whether by accident or design). A third system selects a mare from one of the forty female families listed by an Australian equine aficianado, Bruce Lowe. He developed what was called a "figure guide" for breeders. Mr. Lowe assigned numbers to forty taproot mares of England, based on the classic winners in the tail female line. The number 1 female family would have the most winners, number 2 fewer, and on down the line. Lowe believed that

Mahmoud, imported from England, became one of the great stallions of the Blue Grass.

Bull Lea of Calumet is a proven great stallion. His 'get' have earned millions of dollars.

Eight Thirty, proven stallion, stands at stud at George G. Widener's farm.

Swaps is a newcomer to Blue Grass breeding. Years will tell whether he becomes a great sire.

certain families produced runners and other groups were great sire families. He went so far as to assign definite numbers to the running group and other numbers to the "sire" group. Thus if a breeder wanted a fast runner, he would select family number 1, 2, 3, 4, or 5, while if interested in breeding a good sire for stud, he would select family number 3, 8, 11, 12, or 14.

Actually most of Mr. Lowe's theories have been disproven, but the idea still persists and some breeders take no chances, trying to combine the virtues of all the systems.

According to Joe Estes, editor of *The Blood-Horse,* which might be called the breeder's "bible," the "nick theory" and the Bruce Lowe system "are part of the background of thoroughbred breeding, but nothing in them has anything of practical value, except from the point of view of the salesman, who necessarily seeks to furnish his customers with what they want. Most of them so obviously ignore the principles made clear by modern genetics that it is no longer in order to investigate their dependability. But their dependability has been investigated on numerous occasions and found altogether wanting."

Whether Mr. Estes is right or not, the elaborate breeding systems have supplied after-dinner conversation material for generations of Kentuckians. Some gentlemen have even backed up their belief in the strength of a particular "nick" to the point of dueling over its validity.

The subject of breeding is so uppermost in the thoughts of most Blue Grass citizens that hardly a social occasion goes by without some reference to it. Phrases like, "He certainly stamps his 'get' well" or, "Well, you can try to breed out all the deficiencies but if you've got bad knees, you've got 'em for generations." They tell a story about the distinguished Kentucky family who had a well-known breeder to dinner. After brandy and cigars, the host brought in his handsome ten-year-old to be introduced. The horseman looked at the boy and then back at the father. "Why, Colonel," he exclaimed, "you've outbred yourself."

Being a thoroughbred stallion means having a lot of time to loaf from June first to about the middle of February, but then he goes to work. For the money-earning job of the Blue Grass sire is seasonal. Like professional football, baseball, basketball, and hockey players, he puts in a short but busy spell. The compliment of mares he serves may range from as few as twenty the first season to as many as fifty at the peak of his maturity. Both of these figures are rare and the average will be some thirty to forty mares to cover for the season. The season is primarily determined by the Jockey Club rule which says that every foal becomes a year old on January first. Therefore, to have a well-grown youngster, either to sell as a yearling or to race as a two-year-old, it is essential that he be dropped in the early spring. Another important reason is the ideal Blue Grass weather and pasturage during the spring months, perfect for the newborn foal to grow to healthy maturity.

The stallion's work is no longer as simple nor as inexpensive as it was in the early days of breeding in Kentucky. In the *Kentucky Gazette* for February 16, 1788, there appeared two "at stud" advertisements, one of which reads:

The famous horse *Pilgarlick,* of a beautiful colour, full fourteen hands three inches high, rising ten years old, will stand the ensuing season on the head of Salt River at Captain Abe Irvins, Mercer County, and will cover mares at the very low price of ten shillings a leap, if the money is paid down, or fifteen at the expiration of the season; and twenty shillings the season in cash, or thirty shillings in good trade. *Pilgarlick* was got by the noted imported horse *Janus,* his dam by *Old Silver-eye;* and is the swiftest horse in the district of Kentucke from one to six hundred yards, *Darius* (the property of Berwell Jackson) only excepted.

The other advertised a horse named *Castor.* Both "stood" at a location near the present city of Lexington and actually quite near the Keeneland racecourse.

Times have changed. While *Pilgarlick* stood for twenty shillings the season (about two dollars), a top stallion today commands from $5,000 up. No longer is he hired by the "leap" but serves the mare from one to three times while she is in heat or until she is with foal. Thus the stallion with a "book" of thirty mares is busy almost every day of his one-hundred-day season, and because some mares may have to be brought back time after time, toward the end of the season he can be very rushed indeed. This is where good management helps. As one breeder put it, "We try to give the stallion every opportunity to perform at the peak of his reproductive capacities for the longest possible time." But no matter how good the intentions, the last couple of weeks of the season are hectic ones for the sire.

The booking price, or stud fee of a stallion fluctuates somewhat like that of the buying price of a big league ballplayer. His record as a producer of winners is carefully checked, like a batting average, and happy is the owner who has a successful sire.

Within recent years no one man can afford a top stallion, so these have been syndicated. The syndicate manager starts out by selecting a popular racing stallion to purchase and then sells shares in him at perhaps as much as $40,000 each. He may sell eighteen shares or more, usually reserving two for himself. With the money he purchases the horse for the syndicate, allocates an amount for his upkeep, and is in business. With his two shares he may trade around until he gets to the mare he wants in exchange for one of his shares and breeds her to the stallion with the other. The reason for the syndicate is to give each shareholder a chance to breed to the syndicated horse.

The actual breeding is done in as scientific and routine a way as possible. The men in charge of the stallion and mare work as a team, with one acting as "quarterback" calling the signals. The breeding shed usually has padded walls for the protection of the animals. The mare is restrained with hobbles to keep her from kicking, and with a twitch, a stick with a loop of rope on the end which is twisted around her nose and tightened if she is recalcitrant. With the teams working smoothly, as many as a dozen mares can be bred in a morning to as many stallions.

But although every precaution is taken, breeding is a hazardous business. A pad is usually put on the mare's neck to keep the stallion from biting her deeply. More than once, a mare, in spite of restraints, has attempted to kick the sides out of the breeding shed to avoid mating with a particular stallion. The breeding-shed doors are always left open. There are still a few breeders who prefer outdoor breeding but they are rare and fast becoming extinct. Occasionally a "timid breeder," a stallion who avoids covering the mare, will be bred outdoors. Some years ago a now-famous stallion, *Tom Fool*, backed into a water trough and fell in, trying to avoid a mare. He is now one of the most sought-after of sires. There are also "shy breeders," horses who have trouble getting their mares with foal. But, for the most part, the Blue Grass stallion performs well, and fleet stakes winners all over the world prove it.

In the Blue Grass you may be told what the stallion said to the mare, "It's a business to do pleasure with you."

Show, Harness, and Hunting Horses

WHEN THE HIGH-STEPPING three- and five-gaited show horses prance out at the Junior League Horse Show in the Blue Grass, there is small resemblance to the early Kentucky saddler. Yet the sleek show animals started out as a strictly utilitarian means of transportation. The first horses into Kentucky had to pick their way over the Wilderness Road, which was not a road at all but rather the trace of old buffalo trails and Indian paths. It led through thick brush and lush meadows, over high ravines and into dark, almost impassable, valleys. There was a need for a horse with gaits, one that could go single-foot over the narrow paths, walk carefully along the ridges, and canter easily in the level places without unduly tiring his rider. There was a proverb often quoted in those days, "A good horse never stumbles and a good wife never grumbles."

The settler's family depended upon the horse. He actually became almost one of the family. The training of the horse was as important as the education of the children, and the breeding of fine saddle horses was of first importance to every pioneer. He was handled with pride and bred for use, beauty, and his ability to learn. A man's horse was an extension of his strength. A man's worth was often measured by the horse he rode. The poet Tennyson wrote in *Locksley Hall:*

> He will hold thee, when his passion shall have spent its novel force,
> Something better than his dog, a little dearer than his horse.

Because such a horse had to have speed to outrun Indians and outlaws, the early horse breeders used the thoroughbred. For sturdy, solid dependability and high-stepping action they went to the Morgan horse, which had been developed in New England. The Narragansett pacer supplied an easy ambling gait. But to establish a distinct type of horse a fusion of these strains was needed. It came in the 1840s when a wonder horse was foaled in Bardstown, Kentucky, in the southwestern corner of the Blue Grass. His sire was an imported thoroughbred, *Imported Hedgeford,* his dam, a Kentucky saddler named *Betsy Harrison.* The beautifully formed foal was called *Denmark* and he was to become a great founding sire of the American saddlebred horse. So perfect was the conformation of this stallion that for many years the line that sprang from him was called "The Denmark" horse. Another great foundation sire was *Harrison Chief,* who was descended from the thoroughbred stallion *Messenger.* Now at every horse show, from the Junior League in Lexington to the International Show at Madison Square Garden in New York, almost every American saddle horse traces his ancestry back to the "Denmark" or "Chief" lines.

Slowly the saddlebred type was formed. For generations he drew buggies, traps, and carriages, and bore his master and his mistress on their journeys. But his usefulness faded as other means of transportation evolved. He was at his peak of usefulness and beauty in 1891 when the American Saddle Horse Breeders Association was formed in the Blue Grass. This region is still the home of the registry of these horses.

Almost every great horse farm in the Blue Grass once bred and trained these high-stepping, easy riders. One of them, Castleton, on the old Iron Works Pike and the home of Dodge Stables, breeds and trains many national champions. Some of them—*Primrose Path, Spring Romance, Cora's Mite, Fairy Waters, Belle of the Dell,* and the unparalleled *Wing Commander*—have represented the flower of modern show horses.

Today the saddlebred is strictly a show horse. From a necessity he has turned into a luxury that comparatively few can afford but that gives pleasure by his beauty and grace to millions of horse-show followers. It is doubtful that any other horse gives so much satisfaction to its owner, for his performance is a direct projection of the will of the trainer and rider. As a distinct type of horse, the saddle-bred has been created by man. He looks like the aristocrat that he is. He holds his well-formed, intelligent head high and straight on his long, symmetrical neck. His sturdy back is short and straight. He stands between fifteen and sixteen hands. In motion he gives an exhibition of elegance and controlled power.

But let us see him at the horse show. There he will be shown as a three-gaited horse, as a five-gaited horse, or as a fine harness horse. The three-gaited horse does only the natural gaits. First the foundation gait, the walk, performed in a smooth, graceful, continuous motion. His mane and tail are trimmed and the three-gaited horse is shown only under saddle. His other gaits are the trot, a measured two-beat gait originally developed for road travel, and the canter, a three-beat easy-going gait with the horse held up smartly.

The fine harness horses are driven, in gleaming tack, before a four-wheeled, rubber-tired cart. They are judged at only one gait, the trot.

The five-gaited horse is easy to recognize. He has a full flowing mane and tail, and his rider always wears a derby hat. In addition to the three natural gaits, this carefully trained animal performs the slow gait, a difficult high-stepping, four-beat action, and the rack. The latter is the most difficult of all gaits for the horse. It is a fast four-beat pace that must be slowly and patiently taught. But there are few thrills within the show ring greater than the cry of the judge, when the horses sweep by, of "Let them rack on!"

When the horse shows are over, the trotting-horse season comes to the Blue Grass. The Lexington Trots, dating back to 1891, are the earliest among race meets for harness horses in the United States. The Kentucky Futurity for three-year-old trotters (with $75,000 added) is considered one of the great races of the country and its winner has often become champion three-year-old of the nation. Although only some six per cent of the trotters are foaled in the Blue Grass, approximately half of the United States stakes winners are Blue Grass bred.

As harness racing has become an increasingly more important sport throughout the country, it has also grown within the Blue Grass region. At one time almost every Blue Grass estate bred trotters, along with thoroughbreds, and even today great horse farms are devoted to breeding and training the standardbred horse. Most famous of these is the sprawling Walnut Hall nursery that covers hundreds of acres of rolling Blue Grass pasturage and miles of unspoiled woodland. It is the oldest standardbred horse farm in the world.

The trotting horse, which is now called the Standardbred, got his start in the eastern United States. He was used for road driving and for harness racing in colonial days, and the most important breeding centers evolved in New York State and then in Kentucky. The standardbred comes from the same bloodlines as the thoroughbred, but with the Norfolk trotter developed in Virginia, the Morgan of New England, and pacers of mixed breed added. *Messenger,* who was also a key stallion in the development of the saddle horse, was important in the development

Getting ready for the Lexington Trots, grooms prepare a trotter for the track.

After workout, harness horse is "cooled out" to keep him from catching cold.

Training trotters is a long and difficult chore. They are exercised daily.

of the trotter. His grandson *Mambrino Chief* stood at stud in the Blue Grass, as did three of the four sons of the all-time great, *Hambletonian 10*. They were *Happy Medium, George Wilkes,* and *Dictator. Peter the Great,* another of the legendary stallions, stood in the Blue Grass country and sired *Peter Volo,* who became the sire of the greatest of recent-day stallions, *Volomite.*

At Poplar Hill Farm the brood mares trace back to the world champion *Billy Direct,* who became the head of a line of fleet pacing horses. Almahurst Farm, on the Harrodsburg Pike, is best known for its thoroughbreds today, but it was there that *Greyhound,* another world-champion trotter, was foaled.

Kentuckians take their harness horses seriously, and there are almost as many statues and elaborate headstones over the graves of fleet standardbred trotters and pacers as there are thoroughbred memorials.

Old-timers among the trotting fraternity tell the story of how a group of lady sightseers came to Lexington to see the historic sights and to visit the ante-bellum houses. They went to see the house where Mary Todd Lincoln spent her early years, and in their tour about the town heard that Nancy Hanks was buried nearby. Being curious about the last resting place of Lincoln's mother, they inquired of a group of loafers on Cheapside where the grave of Nancy Hanks was located. They

101

were given directions to proceed four miles east of town on the Winchester Pike. The ladies arrived at Hamburg Place and laid their wreath on the grave of the record-breaking trotting mare, *Nancy Hanks*. Upon returning, one of the ladies remarked, "Those crazy Kentuckians paid an unusual honor to Mr. Lincoln's mother. They put a circle of monuments shaped like a horseshoe around it and a lovely statue of a horse over her grave!"

There is one difference worth noting between the thoroughbred origins of the standardbred trotters and pacers and the thoroughbred running horses. Although the standardbred line could once be traced to the three founding thoroughbred sires, the *Godolphin Arabian*, the *Byerly Turk,* and the *Darley Arabian*, only the Darley line is now alive. It is also the leading thoroughbred line.

The Lexington trotting track today is the home of the famous "Red Mile," considered by harness horsemen perhaps the fastest trotting track in the world. Every fall the important drivers, with their powerful trotters and pacers, descend on the Blue Grass for the big meet. The stable areas swarm with trainers, drivers, and stable boys. In the foggy dawn, trotters and pacers clip off the furlongs against time, while the railbirds stand by, some with stop watches in their hands and others who are said to have clocks in their heads.

Thoroughbred-racing fans can find the trotting track very confusing. On running courses the furlong poles measure the distance starting at the finish line and counting back. The eighth pole is one furlong back from the finish line, the quarter pole a quarter of a mile away. On the trotting track it is reversed. The eighth pole is a quarter mile from the start. Another trotting-horse tip: Never speak of a trotter or pacer "running." He always trots or paces the distance.

Watching the smooth-flowing trotters go around the "Red Mile" in the bright sunshine is like seeing a flight of controlled and numbered arrows shot from a bow: the horse himself the arrowhead, the surrey the shaft, with the driver, spread-legged, seated in the notch.

The horse skims along and the rapid thud of his hoofs approach and fade, then beat toward the finish line. The driver, perched like a mantis inches away from the flying hoofs, keeps his glistening powerhouse under continuous control. He sometimes uses the whip, to which the horse responds as though touched by a hot iron. Into the stretch they pound, driver relaxed but wary, horse showing the strain of maximum effort but keeping his smooth-flowing, restrained gait.

After the race the "hot walkers" take over. These are the stable boys who "cool out" the horse by walking him around until his pounding heart is back to normal and his body heat well reduced. As they walk, he is "watered off" by allowing a few sips of water at well-spaced intervals. The stable area quiets down, and Dalmatian dog mascots sit in front of the wide barn doorways as dark comes to the trotting track.

With the fall of the year comes the time of the hunter, for in the Blue Grass, running the fox to earth is still an important and revered sport played by all the traditional rules. The first rule is a good horse. Some hunters are thoroughbreds, well trained for the hunt. There are also steeplechasers and mixed breeds, but there

Under spreading shade trees two "hot walkers" cool out their harness champions.

After "cooling out," groom admires his charge before taking him to stall for night.

are probably a higher number of pedigreed horses in the ancient Iroquois Hunt, founded by General Roger D. Williams in 1880, than any in the nation.

A traveler to the Blue Grass, should he travel the Richmond Pike between Lexington and Richmond and turn off onto the Boonesboro-Athens road in the early morning, is almost sure to pass fox hunters clopping down the road on their way to join the hunt. If he should happen to traverse the road all the way to Grimes' Mill, home of the Iroquois Hunt, on the first Saturday in November, he would witness a colorful medieval ceremony, the annual "Blessing of the Hounds."

It is a gala occasion, with a gargantuan hunt breakfast similar to, but not exactly like, the old-fashioned Kentucky hunt breakfast that was said to consist of a sirloin steak, a bottle of bourbon, and a hound dog. The steak was for the dog.

Most of the one hundred members of the Iroquois (the membership is now closed) arrive carefully turned out in "pink" coats, top hats or black velvet hunting bowlers, with the men in spotless white breeches. They are a brilliant sight against the ivy-covered mill. The stone mill, built by Philip Grimes in 1803, is now the home of the Iroquois Hunt. The assembled members greet their friends, discuss their horses, and, after breakfast, line up outside the old mill for the "Blessing of the Hounds."

This ritual is very old and is held in honor of Hubert the Huntsman, who, while roving the dense forest near Liége, saw before him a stag with a flaming cross between his antlers. Later, Hubert gave up the chase and became the Bishop of Liége. When he died, he was canonized as St. Hubert and became the patron saint of all huntsmen. While many "blessings" are held on the continent, the ceremony at Grimes' Mill is one of the few in the United States.

An Episcopal bishop officiates, standing upon an ancient millstone before the entrance to the clubhouse. The master and the whippers-in stand by, with the hounds quiet but alert. The bishop wears traditional robes of black, white, and scarlet. He holds a hunting staff in his left hand and a prayer book in the other. Forming a large semicircle are the members of the hunt and their well-behaved horses. As the blessing is given, the hounds remain attentive and the men hold their hats over their hearts. There is no prayer for the fox. According to hunt member Mrs. John Jacob (Rena) Niles, when someone asked whether the fox should not be included, the bishop replied that the fox seemed to be getting along quite well without it.

The ceremony over, the first hunt of the season begins. The riders file over the hills to the area adjacent to Boone's Creek, or nearby open country. The hunt roams, during fall and winter, over a Blue Grass region ten by ten miles that is considered one of the greatest fox-hunting terrains.

This was the country where Daniel Boone settled and made his home. He hunted along the same cedar-clad banks, rode over the green meadows, and saw the grand vistas along the tributaries of the Kentucky River. Now in the crisp autumn afternoons the hounds of the Iroquois are heard giving tongue across the

Member of the Iroquois Hunt is on her way to join meet for ride over Daniel Boone country.

rolling hills, and occasional cheers and tallyhos echo through the valleys. The Iroquois is justly proud of its "Walker" foxhounds, who, like the thoroughbred horse, trace their pedigree back to three great progenitors. These were *Rifle, Fox,* and *Martha.* Like the ancestors of the race horse, they too were imported from England. British and American lines crossed with a Tennessee hound owned by John W. Walker and George Washington Maupin and called Tennessee Lead. From these great dogs the "Walker" line developed.

To give some idea of the degree of importance given the foxhound in the Blue Grass, there is an excerpt from a decision of Judge Eugene Siler of the Kentucky Court of Appeals. The court case involved a foxhound that met his death by falling

Harnessing *Wing Commander,* show-horse champion of champions, at Castleton Farm.

"Blessing of the Hounds" of the Iroquois Hunt. Impressive ceremony is held annually.

Wing Commander puts on a magnificent performance with trainer-driver Earl Teeter.

Beginning of one of the hunts of Iroquois Hunt Club. Morning mist fogs countryside.

into an open well while running the fox. The hound's owner sued the Tennessee Valley Authority for damages. "We are quick to recognize that Stratton proved damages. In the great fraternity of fox hunters, a man's hound is a pearl of considerable price. A common man may freely enjoy without tax or ticket the open air symphony of the melodious harmony of a pack of hounds on a cool, clear night and therein finds that life is good if not somewhat glorious. He often recognizes the distinct voice of his own dog and takes pardonable pride in the leadership of that dog running out there ahead of all the rest. He does not need psychic power to know that 'Old Queenie' is really leading the whole pack. The hound that runs the bushy tail with enthusiasm is just a little lower in the fox hunter's affection than his children. And although habitual fox hunters toil but little and spin but spasmodically, yet Solomon in his palmiest days never had more of a wealth of real happiness than one of these fox hunters, a wealth to which the hounds make a mightly contribution. Sometimes a man goes fox hunting just for the music, sometimes he goes for surcease from unhappy home life, sometimes he goes in pure pride over the 'best dog in the country' . . ."

There is, of course, more to the hunt than the hounds. Among other considerations, there is the farmer whose land is hunted over. The masters of the Iroquois Hunt, in their "hunt ettiquette" brochure, have this to say on the subject: ". . . Although you may feel convinced that it improves wheat, rye, or barley to ride over it, the opinion is not popular, and the fact that some fool has gone ahead is no excuse whatsoever, but makes the matter worse. The spectacle of a lot of men following another's track across a wheat field and killing the young plants which the first had probably injured but slightly is too conducive to profanity to be edifying to any community. You may think that the farmer deems it a privilege to leave his fireside after a hard day's work in the field and travel around half the night in the mud for horses or cattle which have gotten out, or spend days sorting sheep which have got mixed by your leaving his gate open or fences down. You are mistaken. He does not."

He is also eloquent in speaking of the horse and rider: ". . . It is never any excuse that you cannot hold your horse. You have no business to bring out a horse that you cannot hold. If you cannot hold him, go home. If you find you have a kicker, it is imperative that you tie a bright red ribbon near the root of the horse's tail, as a warning to those behind you to keep out of range."

But he is at his best when describing the master of hounds, himself: "The M. F. H. is a great and mystic personage to be lowly, meekly, and reverently looked up to, helped, considered, and given the right of way at all times. His ways are not as other men's ways, and his language and actions are not to be judged by their standard. All that can be asked of him is that he furnish good sport as a rule, and so long as he does that he is amenable to no criticism, subject to no law, and fettered by no conventionality while in the field. He is supposed by courtesy to know more about his own hounds than outsiders and all hallooing, calling, and attempts at hunting them by others are not only bad manners but are apt to spoil sport."

Confederate flags flank magnificent doorway of John Hunt Morgan house.

The Great Houses

HIS HORSE SADDLED and ready beside his front door, John Hunt Morgan was about to join his men for another raid on the Yankees. As he was mounting the speedy mare *Black Bess,* a messenger arrived with the alarming news that a detachment of northern soldiers was on the edge of town, only minutes away. Morgan leaped into the saddle, turned the mare's head toward the broad arched doorway to the parlor, and rode through the house to the kitchen, stopping long enough to lean from the saddle and kiss his mother good-by. Then he cantered off through the kitchen door to join his raiders.

Distinctive cloistered columns rise at Pleasant Lawn on the Versailles-Midway Pike.

Early house above Grimes mill is excellent example of Kentucky's "stone" age.

Whether or not this romantic tale is entirely true, the broad ash floors of the Hunt-Morgan mansion in Lexington would not have given way nor would the thick oak beams have trembled from such an exploit. For the early houses of the Blue Grass country were built to withstand the ravages of man, beast, and nature. From the March day in 1774 when Captain James Harrod and his pioneer band of thirty-one men settled in Harrodsburg, the first town in the Blue Grass, the houses of central Kentucky were built to endure.

Daniel Boone had seen the sturdy oaks, slept under the virgin walnuts and towering hickories. He noted the profusion of ash, beech, maple, and cherry trees. While Boone explored, Harrod and the settlers who followed him built for eternity.

Some of the first log cabins survive, though they were erected rapidly of unseasoned timber. These earliest of Blue Grass dwellings ranged from crude one- and two-room cabins to the "dog trot" type with a covered open area and one or more rooms on either side. The "saddle bag" log house had a wide stone chimney replacing the breezeway between the rooms. Some cabins became the core of more elaborate frame houses, some were used as kitchens when the "big" house was built, others became slave quarters.

The countryside, though a frontier, lent itself readily to the development of a rich way of life. The area was almost uninhabited by Indians, who lived north and south of the Blue Grass and reserved central Kentucky as a hunting preserve. The settlers were therefore free to exploit the excellent climate, the abundance of essential raw materials for construction, and the ideal building sites overlooking the soft rolling hills.

An early horseback-riding circuit judge, describing the countryside at the turn of the century, wrote: "When God made the picturesque, fertile valleys of South-west Virginia, He was just practicing for the Blue Grass Country."

Such vistas inspired the imagination of the early settlers. Their desire to express themselves began to take shape in the design and construction of their homes. Stone houses appeared along the winding branches of the rivers adjacent to the stone quarries. The simplest were constructed of flat surface rock, the more complex of ashlar, square-hewn or thin-dressed stone.

As soon as the early Kentuckians were settled and prospering, they hankered after the conveniences and elegancies they had left behind in Virginia, Maryland, and Pennsylvania.

Slave labor, which included excellent craftsmen, made many of the "great" houses possible. Brick kilns on the plantations transmuted native clay into plain rectangular shapes for walls, molded bricks for cornices, radial bricks for tall columns, and rubbed bricks for archways. Brick colors ranged from deep purple to cherry red. The colors may be seen today, unfaded, in more than four hundred Blue Grass mansions built more than a century ago.

One of the earliest brick dwellings was the Keen place on the Versailles Pike, near Lexington. A magnificent Kentucky colonial-type house, it was built by Francis Keen of Fauquier County, Virginia. It is an unusual house, having two

Ingelside, once one of the Blue Grass' proudest estates, is now a tourist home.

This is the lighted gateway of Hamburg Place. Many standardbreds are buried here.

Modern Blue Grass home is the residence of Rear Admiral Gene and Lucille Markey at Calumet Farm.

Forest Retreat is a combination of a fine old brick dwelling with well-planned modern extension.

front doors but no front hall. The columns are tall and square and there is a broad brick terrace.

Five generations of the Keen family resided here and most of them are buried in the small private cemetery behind the residence. Major John Keen, son of the builder, was aide-de-camp to the Marquis de Lafayette. Both were noted horsemen. Kentuckians were deeply impressed with Lafayette's record-breaking ride

Located near Carlisle, Kentucky, it is the home of Dr. and Mrs. Eslie Asbury.

from New York to Providence, Rhode Island, on a mission for General Washington. It was, therefore, with great fanfare that the entire Blue Grass population turned out to honor the Frenchman when he visited Lexington and his old friends in 1825.

It was a gala fete. The marquis, who was the last surviving major general of the Revolution, arrived at the Keen residence on the spring afternoon of May 15,

The perfect example of the traditional Blue Grass home is this imposing residen

n Rice Road near the Keeneland track. It is the home of Mr. and Mrs. Duval Headley.

1825, and stayed the night. He was greeted by his former companion-in-arms and by another old friend, Colonel Abraham Bowman, commander of the 8th Virginia Regulars in the War of Independence.

Next day the marquis was driven into Lexington and registered at the old Phoenix Hotel. That night all Lexington society, numbering some eight hundred admirers, attended a great ball in his honor. This was no rough frontier gathering of men "half-hoss, half alligator," but a civilized tribute to a distinguished comrade-in-arms.

Typical of the culture of the day was the appointment of young Matthew Harris Jouett, the famous Blue Grass artist, as assistant grand marshal of the Lafayette festivities. Jouett, who had studied with Gilbert Stuart (who called him "Kentucky"), had become the most important painter in the area and was fast becoming known throughout the United States. Young Jouett achieved this despite bitter opposition from his father, who is quoted as saying: "I sent Matthew to college to make a gentleman of him, and he has turned out to be nothing but a damned sign painter." The elder Jouett never completely understood his son's later success, but finally realized there was a good living to be made painting the portraits of the planters and horse breeders of the day. Although Matthew Jouett did

The State Capitol at Frankfort, Kentucky, is especially attractive by moonlight.

not paint horses, he did love to watch them run and was frequently seen at the racecourse. At one time an old servant, Ned, admonished him about betting and pointed out that the racecourse was the work of the Devil. A few days later Jouett surprised Ned up in a tree overlooking the track, watching the thoroughbreds run. "Sir," said Ned quickly, as he climbed down out of the tree, "I am here to catch sinners and to testify against them."

Although the Blue Grass landowners cared enough about portraits of themselves to pay Jouett $25 for a full length, they were more interested in pictures of their horses. By far the most important painter of animals in Kentucky was Edward Troye. Every horse breeder of importance hoped to commission him to create a permanent image of his favorite animal on canvas. J. Winston Coleman, Jr., the contemporary Kentucky historian, quotes Sir Theodore Cook as saying: "In America you had your artists, too. There are the works of Troye, Audubon, and other Americans, but Troye was the best of them all." Troye painted quite a number of portraits of people, mostly of wealthy or important men in the mid-nineteenth century, but his true love seemed to be horses and at their delineation he had no peer.

As a result of Troye's friendship with Alexander Keene Richards of Blue

Oldest college in Kentucky. It was chartered in 1780 by the Virginia Legislature.

Grass Park, an extensive estate near Georgetown devoted to the improvement of the breed, Troye made a memorable trip to the Middle East in 1855–1856, which dramatizes the remarkable devotion to breeding horses then, as now, prevalent in the Blue Grass country. Richards went to Arabia to purchase the fastest Arabian horses he could find to breed to his thoroughbred stock in the Blue Grass. Unfortunately, according to all available records, the experiment was a failure. But although Richards did not go down in history as the greatest breeder of thoroughbreds, the pilgrimage to Arabia did yield some masterpieces: Troye's paintings of the imported Arabian stallions. These were published in 1857 in what is now a very rare eight-page pamphlet.

But by far the most popular and best-known Troye painting was of the great Kentucky race horse, *Lexington*. The association of the horse *Lexington* (named after the Blue Grass city) with one of the great houses of the area is an important one. For *Lexington* was the most important stallion the Blue Grass country has ever known, and Woodburn, where he stood at stud, has the most dramatic history of any of the mansions of the region.

The roots of Woodburn dig deep into the history of the United States. The estate was purchased in 1790, the buyer a young man who had been a good friend and private secretary to Benjamin Franklin. The two thousand acres, more or less,

Elkhorn Creek, famous for its limestone water, meanders through the Blue Grass.

Most horse barns are distinctive but this one has pottery animals climbing on the roof.

were well chosen on the banks of Elkhorn Creek. Because of the dense virgin woodland and its proximity to the creek, called "burn" in Scotland, it may be conjectured that the name "Woodburn" was selected, for the first resident of Woodburn was a Scot, Robert Alexander.

But the importance of Woodburn as a breeding farm began with the son of the builder, Robert Aitchison Alexander, who inherited part of the estate and purchased the remainder from his brother and sister. Robert Alexander loved fine horses. Through his efforts, Woodburn soon became distinguished for its improvement of the breed. In addition to an unsurpassed record for the production of fast race horses, this extensive livestock nursery contributed greatly to the evolution

Loudoun. This medieval castle with tower and turrets still stands in Lexington.

and improvement of the standardbred trotting horse. The great herds of South-down sheep and Durham, Alderney, Ayshire, and Shorthorn cattle that grazed at Woodburn were the talk of the countryside.

Fame came to Woodburn because Robert A. Alexander concentrated on the breeding and racing of thoroughbreds, and the stallion *Lexington* was the corner-stone of its renown.

The purchase of *Lexington* by Robert A. Alexander from Richard Ten Broeck in the year 1856 was a unique transaction. Alexander knew he was ill and yet

John Jacob Niles, a great ballad singer, at his home at Boot Hill. Niles, long a resident of Blue Grass country, has recently published his collection of ballads with music and recordings.

127

Woodburn is one of the great houses of the Blue Grass and is still the residence of the Alexanders.

had planned a trip to England. He did not expect to live to complete the journey. So his contract with Ten Broeck stipulated that he would pay $7,500 on the signing of the contract and the balance of $7,500 if he lived to return from England. He proved to be unduly pessimistic regarding his health, but his judgment in purchasing *Lexington* was sound. Alexander lived eleven more years, long enough to see his stallion become sire of three of the great horses of all time, *Norfolk* and *Asteroid,* who were never defeated, and *Kentucky,* who was only outrun once in his long racing career.

The six tall columns of the classic facade of Woodburn were added after the present house was built in 1848–49, and today the stately homeplace is still the residence of the Alexanders. Inside hang some of the great paintings by Troye of the champions bred at Woodburn. Five were winners of the Kentucky Derby, and the get of the outstanding sires of Woodburn won the Belmont Stakes, the Travers, and the Saratoga Cup nine times!

In a parklike setting,
Mount Brilliant stands
unchanged through the years.

Classically Victorian, this mansion near Paris, Kentucky, is home of Charlton Clay.

Master of the Iroquois Hunt, W. Fauntleroy Pursley, training his Walker foxhounds.

The career of the stallion *Lexington* is closely interwoven with the lives of many of the extraordinary characters of the Blue Grass. He was foaled at The Meadows, where Dr. Elisha Warfield conducted an outstanding breeding establishment. The Meadows was one of the most unusual of Blue Grass mansions. It was built in the Italian Renaissance style on a 123-acre plot on the outer boundary of the town of Lexington. However, the house today is well within the present city limits.

Dr. Warfield, a graduate of the medical college of Transylvania University, was the proud owner of *Boston,* the fastest stallion of his day. He also owned *Alice Carneal,* a racing mare of considerable reputation. From this happy combination came a foal called *Darley*. He was later renamed *Lexington* by Richard Ten Broeck, who purchased him for $2,500 and the promise of a like amount if he won the great stakes race in New Orleans against the highly regarded racing mare *Sallie Waters. Sallie* was the favorite, but Dr. Warfield accepted the offer. "Take him," said Dr. Warfield, "for under those conditions I know I will receive my $5,000. He will win that race." He was right, too.

In 1833 The Meadows was also the scene of an important social event. In February of that year, Mary Jane, the daughter of Elisha Warfield, was married to a young man who became one of Kentucky's greatest and most eccentric citizens, Cassius Marcellus Clay.

Cash Clay took his bride to White Hall, the family home on the Richmond Pike in Madison County. Active in the anti-slavery movement, young Clay established his own newspaper, *The True American,* in Lexington, where his angry editorials soon made him a highly controversial figure throughout the South. After his offices had been attacked and his presses destroyed, he armed his employees and fortified his home.

Clay was a brilliant political speaker who served as United States Minister to Russia during the Civil War. During this period he rebuilt White Hall and incorporated into the rear of the structure the house where he had been born.

Outspoken on almost every subject, Clay has this to say about the ladies of the Blue Grass aristocracy in 1845: "Make up your own beds, sweep your own rooms, wash your own clothes—throw away your corsets and nature will form your own bustles. You will have full chests, glossy hair, rosy complexions, velvet skins, rounded limbs, graceful tournures, eyes of alternate fire, sweet tempers, good husbands, long lives of honeymoons, and—*no divorces.*"

Most picturesque of all the quiet lanes and shady thoroughfares is the old Russell Road, now known as the Russell Cave Pike. It was named for Henry Russell, a Virginia soldier and gentleman, who was killed in Lord Dunsmore's War. A pleasant spring and large pasture along the pike became the site of exciting political rallies that featured barbecues and bourbon.

Adjoining these grounds was Mount Brilliant, a true southern mansion in the Greek Revival style. The central portion of the house was constructed in 1792 by General William Russell, son of Henry Russell. Early travelers through the Blue Grass region described the lavish hospitality and compared the way of life to that in the great châteaux of France.

On Castleton Farm, one of the great Blue Grass estates, Earl Teeter opens specially designed horse gates.

In bonded government warehouse, "leak hunter" regularly examines charred kegs.

The first half of the nineteenth century offered a leisurely way of life, with fine horses playing an important part. A note in *Niles Weekly Register* for January 28, 1815, reads, "Every farmer or planter has his elegant family carriage and his one-horse buggy for himself, with horses and saddles innumerable for the younger branches (of his family) to use when their inclination leads them to gallop uncontrolled from one neighbor's house to another."

One of the great houses they galloped to was Ingelside, a Gothic Romantic type castle with towers, turrets, and spires, and walls of trailing ivy. Ingelside was hand-crafted by slaves who fired the bricks in a kiln in the rear of the house they were constructing. The house was designed and built by John McMurtry, contractor, who became one of Kentucky's finest architects. The owner, Henry Boone Ingels, took McMurtry on a tour of England to gather impressions for the house that was to become Ingelside. The reputation for hospitality at Ingelside was unsurpassed in the entire Blue Grass area and was known throughout the South. Guests often visited for months, and one guest dropped in for a short visit and stayed for ten years. He was finally interred in the family cemetery.

At the close of the nineteenth century, when the glories of Ingelside were fading, Judge James H. Mulligan wrote:

> Hushed are all the voices, faded all the merry throng
> A pall the years have woven, over woodland, tree, and song
> But all come back at even, for the memory still is mine
> As clouds roll back the woodland, tower, turret, lawn and vine
> A day that shines forever, through my recollections glide
> And at twilight comes the picture, of a day at Ingelside.

The great houses of Kentucky deserve a book of their own and this tract can only sketch the framework. But, if possible, they should be seen, for they are living monuments to the individuality and catholic taste of the Kentuckians. Blue Grass houses are not of a type. Tuscan villas, Greek and Gothic Revival, Georgian, Federal, and variations on all of these styles, as well as combinations of them, are typical of the architecture of the region.

An unusual example of various styles may be seen in the home at Pleasant Lawn on the Versailles-Midway Pike. Cloistered columns rise from both front and rear terraces. A Palladian window decorates the angle of one roof side. The columns are arched to form a long colonnade across the rear of the house. It is beautiful, distinctive, and eccentric. Within the house are wall murals painted by Alfred Cohen, an itinerant muralist who attempted to re-create the early history of the state. Being a European, Cohen could not resist using foreign vistas in the background. It is something of a shock to recognize a windmill in Holland in the distance, with a Kentucky colonel and his entourage in the foreground.

There are no murals at Ashland, the ancestral home of Henry Clay, who, in his day, was the first citizen of the Blue Grass. The original house and the present one, which was rebuilt in 1857 on the same site, use octagonal shapes in some areas and have an elliptical stairhall. It is a memorial worth visiting (and is open to the

Built by Henry Clay for his son, this distinctive home combines elegance with simplicity.

public), for the front doorway and Palladian window were recasts of the originals. The house is furnished with original pieces of the period when Clay lived there. It is located within the city limits of Lexington on the Richmond Pike.

For many years there was a sign on the entrance gate of Dixiana Farm, home of Major Barak G. Thomas, that well described the attitude of the Blue Grass estate owner. It read, "Nothing but a good race horse wanted. Agents for the sale of books, patent medicines, sewing machines, wheat farms, and especially lightning rods, not admitted. Visitors who come to my house are always welcome."

On court days, Blue Grass citizens gather around the Court House as they have for generations.

Pink-jacketed jockey stands at the entrance to the Whitney estate on the Paris Pike.

137

Grave of the first pioneer child to be born in Kentucky is at Harrodsburg.

Astride *Black Bess* (now a stallion), John Hunt Morgan,
Confederate hero, looks out on Lexington's Main Street.

Traditions and Legends

THOROUGHBREDS are the gods of the Blue Grass and among these gods
the greatest is *Man o' War*. The thousands who held him in affection and
awe called him "Big Red." Today, thousands still come reverently to the
park area where his grave and a life-size statue are located, just as they did when
he stood at stud on Faraway Farm.

Man o' War has become a legend and a hero in the Blue Grass because he was
not only a winner without equal on the track but also because he was equally
successful as a sire. When his career on the racecourse ended in 1920, he had
broken five American track records. His owner, Mr. Samuel Riddle, could not
sleep one night for worrying how many pounds the handicapper would force the

139

great horse to carry in his one handicap race in order to give the other runners a chance to win. But the handicapper did not make it. Although weighted down with 138 pounds as a three-year-old, "Big Red" won. Almost always, for like most heroes, he once finished second after a bad start. The winner's name was, of course, *Upset*.

From his first race he lived like a horse hero. As a foal and yearling, he was handled by only one man, Alfred Kane. Even in his youth he was handled like the young prince he was. His sire was *Fair Play*, founder of one of the three great American bloodlines, and his dam, *Mahubah*, a speedy mare. Sire and dam are buried side by side with a statue of *Fair Play* above the grave.

However, the paying of homage to the horse did not begin in the Blue Grass but goes far back into the history of the Americas. In the year 1519 a horse actually

Majestic columns rise on Elmendorf, the Widener estate. House was built by Ben Ali Haggin.

Fair Play, sire of *Man o' War*
looks out over Blue Grass country.

Grave of *Regret*, first filly to win the Kentucky
Derby, is on Whitney estate.

Throughout the Blue Grass are parklike areas
where great horses are buried.

141

became a god. The horse was *El Morzillo,* the huge charger of the Conquistador, Hernán Cortés. On one of his journeys of exploration, Cortés visited the Petén area in Guatemala. His friars tried to convert the Indians to Christianity, but they were far more impressed with the horse than with the cross, which had been the Indian's symbol for the god of rain. *El Morzillo* had been disabled on the trip and Cortés was forced to leave him with the primitives.

A few years later a band of Franciscan monks visited Petén on a proselytizing mission. In the temple they were astounded to find a bigger-than-life statue of a huge horse, seated upright with forelegs straight, dominating the house of worship. The Indians explained that the natives from all the countryside had come to view Cortés' great mount and to worship him. They made sacrifices of many fowls and gave offerings of flowers. When *El Morzillo* died, they built a replica of him. Remembering the importance of the cross to the Spanish, they made him their god of thunder, lightning, and rain. So came the horse god to the Americas.

Next to *Man o' War* in the pantheon of legend is *Domino,* whose memorial reads, "Here lies the fleetest runner the American turf has ever known and one of the gamest and most generous of horses." *Domino* was a great runner, but his unique quality was not his speed. It was his gentlemanly generosity. This quality led him to run just fast enough to win. He never embarrassed his competitors by finishing lengths ahead. *Domino* won nineteen out of the twenty-five races of his career, but rarely by more than a head.

It is only a step from a horse as sensitive as *Domino* to the talking horse. The Blue Grass supplies one that also gives the back of the hand to a competing sport. It concerns a young thoroughbred who strayed from his Kentucky pastures and found himself in Chicago. There he took up with a baseball scout who trained him to play baseball and took him to the manager of the Chicago Cubs during one of their losing streaks, with the suggestion that he be put under contract.

"How," said the manager, "can a horse field the ball?" "That's easy," replied the scout. "He wears a glove on his right hoof, so he just canters over, rears up, catches the ball, transfers it from hoof to mouth, and then, with a toss of his head, pegs the ball to the base." "How about batting?" the manager inquired. "Takes the bat in his teeth," said the scout, "gets his eye on the ball, swings that muscular neck, and zowie! What a hitter!"

The manager tried him out in practice and, sure enough, the horse did a great fielding job. He hit pretty well, too. There was a tough game on Saturday, and the manager put him in the line-up. The crowd was astounded at first, but when the horse displayed his skill as a fielder, he was accepted as a competent ballplayer. He came up to bat in the second inning and, after looking over the first couple of pitches, got his teeth into the third one and sent a screaming triple into left center field. He dropped the bat and stood at home plate, bemused.

"Run," shouted the manager, and the fans echoed, "RUN." Slowly the thoroughbred turned to face the crowd. "If I could run," he sighed, "I'd be down at Churchill Downs winning the Kentucky Derby!"

A horse story vouched for by a considerable number of Blue Grass men con-

HERE LIES THE FLEETEST RUNNER
THE AMERICAN TURF HAS EVER
KNOWN, AND ONE OF THE GAMEST
AND MOST GENEROUS OF HORSES.

DOMINO

The grave of the "gentleman horse," *Domino*, is marked by this headstone at Mount Brilliant.

Man o' War statue rises over the grave of *"Big Red."* This area is now a park.

cerns *Himyar,* the sire of *Domino.* He was owned by Major Barak Thomas, breeder, bettor, and Blue Grass squire, who showed him off early one morning to "Billy" Scully, a visiting horse follower. The track was so foggy it was impossible to see the starting point. It was therefore arranged that a groom would strike the rail smartly with a club when the horse came by him, and Scully and Thomas with their stop watches would clock him at the finish line.

As the two horsemen waited in the dense fog, stop watches ready for the sound of the club, the horse rocketed by in the dense mist and at the same moment came the sharp crack of the club hitting the rail. "That," said Scully, "is the fastest horse that ever lived."

Another old-timer, Colonel Phil Chinn of Lexington, back in the dim days when he was known as the sharpest horse salesman in the country, denies the story of having his crew get up very early in the morning, dig up the furlong posts, and place them closer together. He says, "It was a man named O'Brien." The horse being shown that morning broke all existing records.

There are almost as many stories about Colonel Chinn as about horses in the Blue Grass. After a claiming race, it was found that Chinn had claimed a horse that was badly wanted by a character called the "Waco Kid," who was said to have killed five men. "If you take that horse I'm obliged to kill you," said the Kid. But Colonel Chinn claimed away and the Kid, impressed with his courage, backed down.

The colonel was also, he says, a great gambler. On one occasion, he left New York in need of ready cash and telegraphed his friend, W. T. Anderson, another big-time bettor, saying: "COULD USE $25,000.00 PLEASE WIRE REPLY." Upon his arrival in Lexington, the reply was waiting. It read, "ANY-ONE WHO CAN USE $25,000 CAN USE $50,000. MONEY ORDER HEREWITH."

The colonel likes to tell of the time that he almost became the owner of *Man o' War*. He says he bid up to $4,000 but did not like the pedigree. The representative of Samuel Riddle had instructions not to exceed $5,000 and bought him for that figure.

"My motto," he has been quoted as saying, "was 'Let the Yankee Beware.' It was a great pleasure to entertain potential purchasers all night. By morning you could sell them almost anything. They couldn't even see the horses."

One of the giants among horse breeders of the Blue Grass was Colonel E. R. Bradley. He was straight-laced, paternalistic, and the most generous and thoughtful of men. Bradley gave away race horses to his friends, took care of hospital bills for his employees' children, and maintained a private chapel on his farm. He once ran a one-day race meet at a cost of $150,000 for the benefit of the orphanages of Kentucky. He was an easy mark for anyone with a new idea that could be applied to race horses. Colonel Chinn once sold him on short-wave diathermy equipment, and after using it for a few months, Bradley one day asked his manager, Olin Gentry, "Is that stuff doing any good?" "Actually," replied Gentry, "I don't think it's worth a damn." "In that case," said the colonel, "give it to St. Joseph's Hospital."

Bradley was especially concerned about the eyesight of his horses. Many horses do go blind and many others cannot see very well. This made it easy for an oculist to convince the colonel that he could refract the horses' eyes and develop corrective eyeglasses for them. Bradley spent a great deal of money on the "eye doctor." Some lenses were developed and for a time thoroughbreds strolled around the Idle Hour Farm wearing eyeglasses. But it didn't work out. The lenses clouded up or mud bespattered them, and besides their eyelashes interfered.

It was during this period that a saddle maker convinced the colonel that an air blanket, between horse and saddle, would be a great comfort to both horse and jockey. Again Bradley financed the experiments, but the air in the pneumatic saddle blanket shifted with every movement and the jockey found himself sliding from one side to another.

It was not the colonel's concern with eccentric experiments that made him a legend, but his over-all bigness. He was the kind of Blue Grass personality that

145

J. Soule Smith, an early writer in the region, had in mind when he wrote, "It (the Blue Grass) is a poem in itself, and its men and women have the distinct outlines of figures in a Shakespearean drama."

In 1921 Colonel Bradley was all set to win the Kentucky Derby with a three-year-old stallion called *Black Servant*. Bradley had no doubts about the speed and stamina of the horse and bet heavily on him. He entered another fast horse called *Behave Yourself* to act as pacemaker for his favorite. But it did not work out that way. *Black Servant* led all the way around the track, but *Behave Yourself* caught up in the stretch and passed him at the finish. One eyewitness said, "The boy on *Behave Yourself* couldn't seem to hold him at all." Although the colonel was visibly disappointed, he only remarked, "Some washerwoman probably had her two dollars on *Behave Yourself* and her winnings will mean more to her than my losses will to me."

Of all the tales told about Colonel Bradley, none tops the story of the grand Idle Hour Charity Race Meet held on Monday, November 12, 1928. The colonel financed the entire affair, offering a fine card of seven races, six of them with $1,000 added and a feature for two-year-olds with $5,000 added to the purse. Grandstand and boxes were constructed to accommodate two thousand and boxes sold for $50 each. Bleachers were built for seventy-five hundred people, but were entirely inadequate. A total of fifteen thousand horse fans flowed over the Blue Grass and hugged the rail of the private race track.

The meet was a brilliant success. The late Indian summer weather was warm but invigorating. All the races were excellent. *Clyde Van Dusen,* a miniature son of *Man o' War,* won the Orphans Stakes. The colonel had all the new buildings painted in his colors, bright green and shining white. Five colorful tents dotted the grounds, and inside them, white-jacketed attendants served refreshments. Bourbon flowed freely until late in the night and every guest partook of Kentucky's state dish, burgoo, created for this occasion by Colonel James T. Looney, a noted Kentucky chef, who became known throughout the state as The Burgoo King. All the previous night Looney tended his great caldrons, cooking the beef slowly, adding wine at the right moment and in the right quantity. There have been many recipes, but old-timers swear by the one, said to have been originated by a Civil War cook named Gus Jaubert and adapted by Colonel Looney. Burgoo for approximately two hundred people. To prepare for ten divide it by twenty. You'll find that a little more or less makes no difference. Vegetables depend upon availability and substitutions may be made.

> 7 to 10 chickens—3 pounders.
> 10 pounds of lean beef
> 5 pounds of lean veal

Cut meat into chunks. Cut up chickens and sauté lightly in bacon fat. Then put into large (gigantic) kettle and cover with water. Add 36 onions, 5 or 6 bunches of celery tops, and a couple of bunches of parsley. Also add 5 or 6 chopped red peppers, a handful of black pepper, and a couple of bay leaves. Salt this gener-

Ornate monument to anti-slavery champion and ambassador, Cassius Marcellus Clay.

ously. Let this brew simmer for about six hours on a slow fire. The chicken meat should be falling off the bones.

Then chop up 3 dozen carrots, a dozen turnips, 2 dozen bunches of celery stalks, 12 pounds of okra, two dozen potatoes, 3 cabbages, and sauté them in butter. Cool the meat and remove the bones. Add the sautéed vegetables and 3 dozen peeled tomatoes. Simmer for a couple more hours to a thick, well-mixed consistency. Finally, add cooked corn, cut off the cob (optional) an hour before ladling it up. Important: As the burgoo cooks down, add red wine to keep it semisolid. It should take 2 or 3 bottles of claret.

Colonel Bradley was so pleased with Looney's concoction that he named a newborn foal after him, and the 1932 Kentucky Derby winner was *Burgoo King*.

There may be grounds for argument about burgoo being the great Blue Grass cuisine, but there is none as to bourbon whiskey. It is the most important drink of the region, born and nurtured in Bourbon County and consecrated back in 1825 by Chief Justice Marshall, who composed the famous couplet:

In the Blue Grass region, a paradox was born,
The corn was full of kernels, and the Colonels full of corn.

147

But bourbon got its start long before 1825. As early as 1790, Jacob Spears was making whiskey near Paris, in the heart of Bourbon County. (It is sad that there is no bourbon made in Bourbon County today). A year earlier, it is recorded, the Reverend Elijah Craig, a Baptist minister, made a very good whiskey in that area. In those early days, whiskey was considered as essential as meat or flour. It was used for medicinal purposes and one scribe of the period said, "A man can run, jump, and shoot better after one drink of that noble fluid." Local whiskey was served in the colorful inns that went by such names as "The Buffalo," "The Indian Queen," "The Sheaf of Wheat," and "Postlethwaite's Tavern."

The French Consul to the United States, André Michaux, traveled through the Blue Grass in 1793 and reported, "Horses and lawsuits comprise the usual topics of conversation. If a traveler happens to pass by, his horse is appreciated. If he stops, he is presented with a glass of whiskey and then asked a thousand questions."

In the early days, whiskey was so strong and so raw it was strictly a man's drink. There is an early story about a northern surveyor who met a Kentucky woodsman carrying a jug of whiskey and a rifle. The woodsman pushed the jug into the stranger's hands and then stepped back and aimed his gun at the frightened surveyor. "Take a drink," he commanded. The northerner gulped down a few swallows of the fiery liquid. The Kentuckian took back the jug and handed his gun to the stranger. "Now," he insisted, "you make me take a drink!"

A few years ago, the Louisville police department got a call complaining that a drunken horse was endangering traffic on a rural road. A squad car was dispatched. Sure enough, at the spot described, a horse was staggering down the road. The officer smelled the horse's breath and there was no doubt that the animal was drunk. He reported over the radio that he had made contact with the horse and asked further instructions. "Take him into custody," came the order. The officer did his best to comply and succeeded in following the horse for some distance when it went up a driveway and lay down in front of a house. A light went on and a man came to the door and looked out. "Is that your horse?" asked the officer. "That it is," was the answer. The policeman gave him a summons for creating a nuisance and disturbing the peace, and then asked: "What are you going to do about that horse?" "Going to shoot him," was the reply. "Any horse that will get dead drunk and stay out all night ain't worth keeping."

How does a horse get drunk? Well, in Kentucky there are still a number of rugged individuals who do not believe that a man should be deprived of the right to make his own whiskey. In spite of laws and revenue officers, the moon still shines on the moonshine stills along some of the Blue Grass creeks. A horse with decadent taste sometimes stumbles onto some of the sour mash waste left after the liquor has been distilled and gets very drunk indeed. However, this is most unusual, since most horses hate the taste of alcohol and will not even drink from a stream that has been polluted by waste matter from a still. One revenue officer achieved a considerable reputation for himself by tracing stills along the creeks where his horse refused to drink.

Over the years bourbon whiskey has been improved by various methods of refining and aging. It was discovered that by leaving the whiskey in oak kegs that were charred on the inside the flavor was greatly enhanced. Old-timers refer to "drinking whiskey" and "sippin' whiskey," the latter properly aged.

Today all bourbon whiskey is aged, though some gets much more aging than others. Much of the liquor produced in Kentucky is "bottled in bond," which means that it is stored in bonded warehouses for a minimum of four years and a maximum of eight, and that the bourbon tests at 100 proof, or fifty per cent alcoholic content. This guarantees a strong and full-bodied whiskey.

"Kentucky" Gus Petty, headwaiter at the Keeneland racecourse clubhouse, avows: "That burgoo and bourbon combination is the finest, but the old ones can't stand so much today and the young ones can't afford it!"

Bourbon is indubitably Kentucky, but not so with another of the most important Blue Grass traditions, the mint julep. The state of Virginia has long laid claim to the julep, but in that state it is simply a drink, albeit a good one, while in the Blue Grass the julep is a way of life. The following letter was written by Mr. Hogan Trammel, Administrative Assistant of the Lexington Chamber of Commerce to a misguided lady of California who inquired about the mint julep:

"You cannot mean what you said in your letter of October 17, about using Gin in a MINT JULEP. When I read your letter tears came to my eyes. The very idea of using anything but sugar, mint, ice, and KENTUCKY WHISKEY, in a MINT JULEP made me heartsick. We are enclosing a recipe given to us by the now famous Colonel Henry Watterson. The dignity of the JULEP is great, and commands the respect of everyone who has sniffed its fragrant aroma, and sipped its sweet nectar. . . . .

"Please accept this little piece of advice; be humble before this drink, you must respect it, you must live your life in the manner it demands—easy. If you don't take it easy, you'll be the drunkest one woman that ever staggered a stagger."

Every Blue Grass host has his own variation of the julep, but they are so minor as to be almost indistinguishable. A considerable number of people use Colonel Henry Watterson's recipe:

"Take a silver goblet—one that holds a pint—and dissolve a lump of loaf sugar in it with not more than a tablespoon of water. Take one mint leaf, no more, and crush it gently between the thumb and forefinger before dropping it into the dissolved sugar. Then fill the goblet nearly full to the brim with shaved ice. Pour into it all the bourbon whiskey the goblet will hold. Take a few sprigs of mint leaves and use for decorating the top of the mixture, after it has been well frappeéd with a spoon. Then sip, but don't use a straw."

But few mint julep goblets actually hold a full pint. Traditionally, the julep cup is silver and is usually decorated with engraved or relief designs. The Keeneland racecourse awards hand-wrought julep cups to winners of stakes races, and some Blue Grass farmowners have assembled full sets of the handsome goblets.

The mint julep may be imbibed at any time, though the cool of the evening is when most are served. It is a simple drink, as are most great ones, and the only ingredients ever used are mint, sugar, bourbon, and water. There are few pleasures equal to that of swaying gently in an old-fashioned rocking chair, looking out at the yearlings across the white fences from the broad veranda of a Blue Grass home. The mint julep is cold and frosty to the touch, and the true julep drinker never uses a straw but savors the cool bourbon-mint taste on his lips and tongue while sniffing the refreshing bouquet.

No writer is ever likely to exceed the vision of the julep as seen by Soule Smith, a flowery but imaginative newspaperman of the late nineteenth century. This is his classic recipe:

". . . The bourbon and the mint are lovers. In the same land they live, on the same food are fostered. The mint dips its infant leaf into the same stream that makes the bourbon what it is. The corn grows in the level lands through which small streams meander. By the brookside the mint grows. As the little wavelets pass, they glide up to kiss the feet of the growing mint, the mint bends to salute them. Gracious and kind it is, living only for the sake of others. The crushing of it only makes its sweetness more apparent. Like a woman's heart, it gives its sweetest aroma when bruised. Among the first to greet the spring, it comes. Beside the gurgling brooks that make music in the pastures it lives and thrives. When the Blue Grass begins to shoot its gentle sprays toward the sun, mint comes, and its sweetest soul drinks at the crystal brook. It is virgin then. But soon it must be married to Old Bourbon. His great heart, his warmth of temperament, and that affinity which no one understands, demands the wedding. How shall it be?

"Take from the cold spring some water, pure as angels are; mix with it sugar till it seems like oil. Then take a glass and crush your mint within it with a spoon —crush it around the borders of the glass and leave no place untouched. Then throw the mint away—it is a sacrifice. Fill with cracked ice the glass; pour in the quantity of bourbon which you want. It trickles slowly through the ice. Let it have time to cool, then pour your sugared water over it. No spoon is needed, no stirring is allowed—just let it stand a moment. Then around the brim place sprigs of mint, so that the one who drinks may find a taste and odor at one draught. When it is made, sip it slowly. August suns are shining, the breath of the south wind is upon you. It is fragrant, cold, and sweet—it is seductive. No maiden's kiss is tenderer or more refreshing; no maiden's touch could be more passionate. Sip it and dream—you can not dream amiss. Sip it and dream, it is a dream itself. No other land can give so sweet a solace for your cares; no other liquor soothes you so in melancholy days . . ."

Along with mint juleps go the traditional horse-farm parties. Although not so many parties are given as in the nineties and the pre-War (War—between the states, that is) days, they are just as opulent and just as gay. In retrospect, the social gatherings in the early twenties of Mrs. Clarence LeBus and Clara Bell Walsh (Mrs. Julius Walsh) sound like the greatest parties of all time, but the parties today given by the Markeys of Calumet, the Hancocks of Claiborne, the Combs of Spendthrift, and Mrs. Helen Carruthers of nearby Versailles, Kentucky, can match the early ones in style and spirit.

Horse motif appears throughout the Blue Grass country. These three indicate a long-established liquor store and two popular restaurants.

Mrs. Carruthers says with pride that she has never given a "cocktail" party. "When I have guests, I like them enough to have them to dinner." Mrs. Carruthers also frowns on the idea of buffet dinners. "I will never get used to the idea of having to eat off my knees," she said. "I want my guests to sit at the table, not on the stairway." Dinner parties at her home are sit-down affairs. "I don't give as big parties as I used to," she said. "I limit my guests to the dining-room table and it only seats twenty-five to thirty." During the Keeneland race meet and the spring yearling sales, she does admit to a dinner party every night, "or maybe," she said, "it just seems like every night. All this may sound formal to you," she continued, "but actually all my house guests come to my room and sit around all over the place at breakfast time. We have a very gay time during the sales. I put all the male guests on the top floor and it is quite a group—bankers, jockeys, trainers, brokers, and even actors. Racing makes strange bedfellows!" she concluded.

The party tossed by Lucille and Gene Markey of Calumet Farm for the Aly Khan in the spring of 1958 was entirely in the Blue Grass tradition. The guest list included not only the Blue Grass aristocracy but also a considerable portion of Who's Who in international racing circles. After dinner and far into the night, music was supplied by Bill Smith's all-Negro gut-bucket jazz band. The guests supplied their own entertainment. Smith's jazz band is a Blue Grass institution that had died out but was revived when Leslie Combs, who remembered Smitty and his band from dances in his youth, found Smith working in a restaurant and agreed to help him buy instruments to revive his old-time jazz band. Smitty bought a saxophone, gathered together four musicians, and was in business again. No one in the outfit can read music, but the primitive sounds they blow, squeeze, strum, and beat out of their instruments are the joy of the Blue Grass hosts.

At every party, Smitty likes to dedicate a number to his employer and to the honored guest. He knows the favorite tune of the host as a rule, and toward the middle of the evening he is likely to address the party thus: "I am now gonna play 'Mr. Sandman' for Miss Lucille." At the party for Prince Aly Khan, he was at a loss both for a number and for a way to address the prince. He solved the problem by selecting his own favorite number and added to the lore of the Blue Grass by solemnly announcing, "The next number is for you, Prince—'Shake It and Break It, and Hang It on the Wall!'"

But there are few big Blue Grass parties without the indispensible services of Mrs. Una Quarles, Lexington's top-notch cook, caterer, and social essential. "It's getting so you have to make a date for your party a year ahead," said Mrs. Duval Headley, wife of the president of the Keeneland track. "I told her I wanted to have a party in the spring and she said, 'Well, I can let you have it the last Saturday in May.' She is so overworked that some of her clients got together and planned to send her on a holiday before the beginning of the Derby season so she would be in good condition to handle the press of parties."

In direct contrast to the food and decoration and succulent food furnished by Mrs. Quarles, horsemen in search of male companionship used to make an occasion of going to Johnnie Furlong's hole-in-the-wall restaurant on Limestone Street in the heart of Lexington. Johnnie served the finest "chittlins" in the region. The hog entrails were cooked in a large lard can and the cleanliness of the "kitchen" was such that one patron suggested that if Johnnie's cook could be induced to take a bath the health department would raise the sanitation rating from a "D" to a "C" card.

Two other favorite dishes deserve a place in traditional Blue Grass eating. One is lamb fries, the gonads of the lamb, and rooster fries (a speciality of the chef at the Lafayette Hotel), which comprise the same toothsome, though tiny, organs of the rooster. Johnnie Furlong is still alive but his restaurant has changed hands. The chef at the Lafayette Hotel still occasionally telephones some of the old-timers when he has rooster fries available.

In the comfortable quarters of the Thoroughbred Club of America in Lexington's Phoenix Hotel, one may pick up an endless supply of "true legends." A few years ago, it is said, a Kentucky judge failed to grant a divorce because of a horse. The wife, insisting her husband was neglectful, complained, "Judge, he even completely forgot the date of our wedding." "How about that?" the judge asked. "Of course I remembered it," said the defendant. "It was the day *Gallant Fox* won the Wood Memorial."

Or the tale about a member of the congregation of a Lexington church. He requested the pastor to ask the congregation to pray for Miss Annie Bell. The parson complied and the next Sunday, before services, asked the gentleman if he wanted Annie Bell remembered again. "No, thank you kindly," he said. "She won last Wednesday at 7 to 1."

There is the story of Father Stephen Theodore Badin, who was walking down the Bardstown Road with a saddle on his back. He was met by a Presbyterian minister who stopped his buggy to ask, "Where is your horse, Father?" "He died a way back on the road," the priest replied. "And did you give him absolution before he died?" persisted the minister. "No, it would have been useless. The silly animal turned Presbyterian *in articulo mortis,* and went straight to hell."

In Glasgow, Kentucky, a woman parked her convertible on the edge of the fair grounds and a hungry horse ate the tasty vinyl plastic top off, and in New Haven, Kentucky, a man and horse fell into an open gravel pit and the horse ate most of his hair off during the night they were helplessly wedged together. "She practically scalped me," he said. "I could feel her teeth scraping the bone. Sounded like she was chewing on an ear of corn."

Best known of all the Blue Grass stories concerns *Black Bess,* the speedy mare that carried John Hunt Morgan, the raider and scourge of the Yankees, on his lightning raids. Long after his death, the United Daughters of the Confederacy, the Sons of Confederate Veterans, and other patriotic groups raised the necessary money and employed a sculptor to create a statue of Morgan mounted on his famous mare. The sculptor spent a year on the statue. When the work was unveiled, a gasp of horror went up from the crowd. It was Morgan to the life and the likeness of the good mare *Bess* was unmistakable—up to a point—for the sculptor had supplied her with *all* the physical equipment of a stallion!

There are also many stories about little Isaac Murphy, the Negro jockey considered by the old school of Kentucky horsemen the greatest rider of all times. Murphy won his first race at Crab Orchard, Kentucky, in 1875 when he weighed only seventy-four pounds. His weight ultimately reached ninety-five pounds and stayed there most of his life. Murphy, for fifty years, was the only jockey to win three Kentucky Derbies, and his record of 628 races won, out of a total of 1,412 mounts, still stands. At one meet in 1879 which featured four races, Murphy won them all, two of them with the same horse. He rode with long stirrups and, according to a newsman of the time, "would just lay down on the horse's neck and bring him home." With the fast horse, *Leonatus,* he said, "I won eight races without lifting my hands."

Murphy was a highly respected gentleman, as well as a top-flight jockey. He owned a fine home on East Third Street in Lexington, entertained prodigally, and owned paintings of many of his famous mounts. He was only injured once, when his horse tumbled over a horse that had fallen. Although slightly hurt, Murphy managed to drag the other jockey in to safety under the rail.

Of the legendary gamblers, Riley Grannon was the greatest. He was born in Bourbon County and, from a slow start, ran up at least half a dozen fortunes that he won and lost with equal equanimity. In one of his down-and-almost-out periods, he was going through his clothing to send a suit to the cleaners. In a forgotten pocket he found a fifty-dollar bill. Grannon immediately took off for the track and ran the fifty up to twenty thousand in an afternoon. After a particularly big killing, Riley brought his winnings to Lexington, where he opened the Navarre Cafe, named after a great racer, *Henry of Navarre,* Grannon made the restaurant the finest in the region and claimed that he could serve anything that could be found in New York. Perhaps this was why the Navarre failed. Grannon said, "Lexington people never want anything but half a dozen fried or half a dozen raw."

The great gambler went broke for good in California when only forty years old. From there he went to Rawhide, Nevada, where he died. The account of his funeral includes all the stock props and characters. The body in a rough coffin, the alcoholic minister awakened from his hangover to preach the funeral sermon, miners, prostitutes, gamblers, and bartenders in attendance. The sermon was long but it ended with these words:

> Riley Grannon lived in a world of sport. My words are not minced, because I am telling what I believe to be true. It was a world of sport, sometimes hilarity, sometimes worse. He left the impress of his character upon us all, and through the medium of his financial power he was able with his money to brighten the lives of all who knew him.
>
> He wasted his money, so the world says; but did it ever occur to you that the men and women and the class

upon whom he wasted it were yet men and women? A little happiness brought into their minds means as much to them as happiness carried into the lives of the straight and good. If you can take one ray of sunshine into the night life and thereby carry a single hour of happiness, you are a benefactor. Riley Grannon did this.

God confined not his sunbeams to the nourishing of potatoes and corn. His scattering of sunshine was prodigal. Contemplate—He flings the auroral beauties 'round the cold shoulders of the North. He hangs quivering pictures of the mirage above the palpitating heart of the desert. He scatters the sunbeams like scattered gold upon the bosom of a myriad of lakes that gem the robe of nature. He spangles the canopy of night with star jewels and silvers the world with the reflected beams from on high. He hangs the gorgeous curtain on the Occident across the sleeping room of the sun.

God wakes the coy maid of the morning to step timidly from her boudoir of darkness to climb the steep of the Orient, to fling wide the gates of morning and trip over the landscape, kissing the flowers in her flight. She arouses the world to herald with its music the coming of her king, who floods the world with effulgent gold.

These are wasted sunbeams, are they? I say to you that men and women who by the use of money or power are able to smooth one wrinkle from the brow of human care, to change one man's sob into song, or to wipe away a tear and place in its stead a jewel of joy, are public benefactors. Such was Riley Grannon.

The time has come to say good-by. For the friends and loved ones not here to say the word let me say "good-by, old man." We will try to exemplify the spirit you left as we bear the grief at our parting. Words fail me here. Let those flowers, Riley, with their petaled lips and perfumed breath, speak in beauty and fragrance those sentiments too tender for words. Good-by!

The minister's speech sounds very like the flowery prose of Soule Smith quoted previously on the mint julep. But whether Riley Grannon's obituary was invented does not really matter. It is an impressive statement about a great gambler.

Soule Smith was the prose poet of the Blue Grass and one more short quotation from him is irresistible: "Here I shall quit my theme, the land I will not, cannot quit until an angel wing shall brush me from this world. Then in the heart of old Kentucky shall my body lie at rest, while my spirit broods upon the Blue Grass land."

155

ACKNOWLEDGMENTS

The tradition of hospitality still thrives in the Blue Grass Country. The author is especially indebted to the following ladies and gentlemen: Mr. J. A. Estes and the staff and management of *The Blood-Horse* Magazine; Mrs. Amelia Buckley of the Keeneland Library; Dr. J. Winston Coleman, Jr., distinguished Kentucky historian; Mr. Sidney Hertzberg; Mr. and Mrs. Duval Headley; Mr. and Mrs. Leslie Combs, II, of Spendthrift; Mr. and Mrs. A. B. Hancock of Claiborne; Mrs. Helen Carruthers of Versailles; Colonel Phil Chinn of Lexington; Mr. and Mrs. Barry Bingham of Louisville; Mr. and Mrs. John Jacob Niles of Boot Hill, Fayette County; Mr. Roscoe Goose of Louisville; "Kentucky" Gus Petty; Mr. Ed Wilder and Mr. Hogan Trammel of the Lexington Chamber of Commerce; Miss Mary Jane Gallagher; Mr. and Mrs. Cary Robertson of Anchorage; Miss Sharon Smith of Lafayette, Indiana; Dr. and Mrs. Eslie Asbury of Forest Retreat; Charlton Clay of Bourbon County; Dr. Charles E. Hagyard of Lexington, and Mr. W. T. Bishop of Keeneland Race Track. The author also wishes to thank the Jockey Club, The Museum of Natural History, The Frick Museum and Art Gallery, Mr. Michael Smith, and Mrs. Joseph (Bay) Wasserman for their cooperation.

BIBLIOGRAPHY

ANDERSON, JAMES DOUGLAS. *Making the American Thoroughbred.* Norwood, Massachusetts: The Plimpton Press, 1916.

BRUCE, SANDERS D. *The American Stud Book.* 2 vols. New York: Sanders D. Bruce, 1873.

CLAY, CASSIUS M. *The Life of Cassius Marcellus Clay: Memoirs, Writings and Speeches.* Cincinnati: J. Fletcher Brennan & Co., 1886.

CLAY, MRS. JOHN M. *The Sport of Kings.* New York: Broadway Publishing Company, 1912.

COLEMAN, J. WINSTON, JR. *Edward Troye: Animal and Portrait Painter.* Lexington. Winburn Press, 1958.

———— *Old Homes of the Blue Grass.* A photographic Review by Richard Garrison with an introduction by Sidney S. Combs and a Commentary by J. Winston Coleman, Jr. Lexington: The Kentucky Society, 1950.

———— *Stage Coach Days in the Blue Grass.* Louisville: The Standard Press, 1935.

DENHARDT, ROBERT MOORE. *The Horse of the Americas.* Oklahoma: University of Oklahoma, 1949.

EDGAR, PATRICK NISBETT. *American Race—Turf Register & Stud Book.* 2 vols. New York: Henry Mason, 1833.

ESTES, BETSY WORTH. "A Study of the Relationship Between Temperament of Thoroughbred Broodmares and Performance of Offspring." *Journal of Genetic Psychology,* 1952.

———— "Temperament." Lexington: *The Blood Horse,* October 28, 1950.

ESTES, J. A. and PALMER, JOE H. *An Introduction to the Thoroughbred Horse.* Lexington: The Blood Horse, 1943.

HAMILTON, EDITH. *Mythology.* Boston: Little, Brown and Company, 1942.

HATCH, ALDEN and KEENE, FOXHALL. *Full Tilt, the Sporting Memories of Foxhall Keene.* New York: The Derrydale Press, 1938.

HERVEY, JOHN. *Racing in America.* 2 vols. New York: Privately printed, 1944.

KNIGHT, THOMAS A. and GREENE, NANCY LEWIS. *Country Estates of the Blue Grass.* Cleveland: The Britton Printing Company, 1904.

LANCASTER, CLAY. *Ante-Bellum Suburban Villas and Rural Residences of Fayette County Kentucky and Some Outstanding Homes of Lexington (An Architectural Map and Explanatory Booklet).* Lexington: Privately printed by the Thoroughbred Press, 1955.

———— *An Architectural Ramble in Historic Ante-Bellum Lexington (A Bird's-eye View).* Lexington: The Foundation for the Preservation of Historic Lexington and Fayette County, 1956.

MASON, RICHARD. *The Gentleman's New Pocket Farrier.* Richmond: P. Cottom, 2nd ed., enlarged, 1820.

NEWCOMB, REXFORD. *Old Kentucky Architecture.* New York: William Helburn, Inc., 1940.

PALMER, JOE H. *This Was Racing.* New York: A. S. Barnes, 1953.

Porter's Spirit of the Times. New York: 1856–59.

PRESCOTT, WILLIAM H. *History of the Conquest of Mexico.* New York: Henry Holt & Co., 1922.

SCOTT, WILLIAM BERRYMAN. *History of Land Mammals of the Western Hemisphere.* New York. MacMillan, 1937.

SMITH, J. SOULE. *Art Work of the Blue Grass Region of Kentucky.* Oshkosh: Art Photogravure Company, 1898.

THOMPSON, LAWRENCE SIDNEY. *Kentucky Tradition.* Hamden, Conn.: Shoe String Press, 1956.

WELLMAN, MANLY W. *The Life and Times of Sir Archie.* Chapel Hill: The University of North Carolina Press, 1958.

WILLIAMS, MOYRA. *Horse Psychology.* New York: A. S. Barnes, 1957.

Wilke's Spirit of the Times. New York: 1859, 1874.

Kentucky Gazette. Lexington, Kentucky.

Index